STEP-BY-STEP

Baking for Beginners

QUICK & EASY

Publisher's Note: Raw or semi-cooked eggs should not be consumed by babies, toddlers, pregnant or breastfeeding women, the elderly or those suffering from a chronic illness.

Publisher & Creative Director: Nick Wells
Senior Project Editor: Catherine Taylor
Editorial: Esme Chapman
Art Director: Mike Spender
Layout Design: Jane Ashley
Digital Design & Production: Chris Herbert

Special thanks to Laura Bulbeck and Frances Bodiam.

FLAME TREE PUBLISHING
6 Melbray Mews, Fulham,
London SW6 3NS, United Kingdom
www.flametreepublishing.com

This edition published 2016
Content from this book was previously published as *Baking*.

Copyright © 2016 Flame Tree Publishing Ltd

18 20 19
3 5 7 9 10 8 6 4 2

ISBN: 978-1-78361-955-9

Printed in China

All images are courtesy of Flame Tree Publishing Limited except the following which are courtesy of Shutterstock.com and © the following contributors: 9 Sea Wave; 10 tommaso lizzul; 11 Joerg Beuge; 13 Ildi Papp; 16 Douglas Freer; 19 Marie C Fields; 22 Christopher Elwell; 25 Joe Gough; 12b Dream79; 12t bitt24; 17b Dirk Ott; 17t, 29b bonchan; 18b Africa Studio; 18t sutsaiy; 20, 39t Innershadows Photography; 26b Raffaella Calzoni; 26t Ollgga; 27t Domenic Gareri; 29t Audi Dela Cruz; 30, 31t Dzinnik Darius; 32t istetiana; 35b CandyBox Images; 39b Brent Hofacker; 41b margouillat photo; 41t Maryna Pleshkun; 42b spectrumblue; 42t violeta pasat; 43b Swellphotography; 43t Ev Thomas; 8, 28 Gayvoronskaya_Yana.

STEP-BY-STEP

Baking for Beginners

QUICK & EASY

General Editor: Gina Steer

**FLAME TREE
PUBLISHING**

CONTENTS

———◆———

ESSENTIALS

Everybody loves the tempting aroma and delicious taste of home baking, so it's definitely a desirable skill to have under your belt! Before you roll up your sleeves and start cooking, check out this essentials section which covers everything you'll need to know to be a great baker. From essential ingredients and equipment to basic techniques and recipes, this section will have you feeling confident and prepared. Also included is a useful list of culinary terms and conversions.

ESSENTIAL INGREDIENTS

*T*he quantities may differ, but basic baking ingredients do not vary greatly. Let us take a look at the baking ingredients which are essential.

Fat

Butter and firm block margarine are the fats most commonly used in baking. Others can also be used such as white vegetable fat, lard and oil. Low-fat spreads are not recommended as they break down when cooked at a high temperature. Often, it is a matter of personal preference which fat you choose when baking, but there are a few guidelines that are important to remember.

∾ **Butter and Margarine** Butter is the fat most commonly used in cake-making, especially in rich fruit cakes, and it gives a distinctive flavour to the cake. You can use unsalted butter in delicate cakes and icings, but ordinary salted butter or slightly salted is better for general baking. Some people favour margarine which imparts little or no flavour to the cake. As a rule, firm margarine and butter should not be used straight from the refrigerator but allowed to come to room temperature before using (known as 'softened'). Also, it should be beaten by itself first before creaming or rubbing in. Soft margarine, sold in tubs, is a quick and easy fat that can be used straight from the refrigerator and is ideal for one-stage recipes.

∾ **Oil** Light oils, such as vegetable or sunflower, are sometimes used instead of solid fats. However, if oil is used, care should be taken – it is vital to follow a specific recipe as the proportions of oil to flour and eggs are different and these recipes will need extra raising agents.

- **Fat in Pastry-making** Fat is an integral ingredient when making pastry; again, there are a few specific guidelines to bear in mind. For shortcrust pastry, the best results are achieved by using equal amounts of lard or white vegetable fat with butter or block margarine. The amount of fat used is always half the amount of flour. Other pastries use differing amounts of ingredients. Pâte sucrée (a sweet flan pastry) uses all butter with eggs and a little sugar, while flaky or puff pastry uses a larger proportion of fat to flour and relies on the folding and rolling during making to ensure that the pastry rises and flakes well. When using a recipe, refer to the instructions to obtain the best result.

Flour

- **Flour Types** We can buy a wide range of flour, all designed for specific jobs. Strong ('bread') flour, which is rich in gluten, whether it is white (shown top left of the picture here) or brown (this includes wholemeal – shown top right – granary and stoneground) is best kept for bread.

  00 flour is designed for pasta-making and there is no substitute for this flour.

  Ordinary plain flour is best for cakes, biscuits and sauces as it absorbs the fat easily and gives a soft light texture. This flour comes in plain white, self-raising (which has the raising agent already incorporated, shown bottom left of the picture here) and wholemeal varieties (wholemeal self-raising, shown bottom right). Plain flour can be used for all types of baking and sauces.

- **Flour and Raising Agents** If using plain flour for scones or cakes and puddings, unless otherwise stated in the recipe, use 1 teaspoon baking powder to 225 g/8 oz plain flour. With sponge cakes and light fruit cakes, where it is important that an even rise is achieved, it is best to use self-raising flour because, since the raising agent has already been added, there is

Essential Ingredients

no danger of using too much – which can result in a sunken cake with a sour taste. There are other raising agents that are also used. Some cakes use bicarbonate of soda with or without cream of tartar (both these compounds are typical ingredients in baking powder), blended with warm or sour milk. Whisked eggs also act as a raising agent as the air trapped in the egg ensures that the mixture rises. Generally, no other raising agent is required.

❧ **Other Flour** There is even a special light sponge flour designed especially for whisked sponges. Also, it is possible to buy flours that contain no gluten and so cater for coeliacs. Buckwheat, soya, rice and chick pea flours are also available.

Eggs

When a recipe states 1 egg, it is generally accepted this refers to a medium egg. Over the past few years, the grading of eggs has changed. For years, in the UK, eggs were sold as small, standard and large, then this method changed and they were graded in numbers with 1 being the largest. The general feeling by the public was that this system was misleading, so now we buy our eggs as small, medium and large. Due to the slight risk of salmonella, all eggs are now sold date-stamped to ensure that the eggs are used in their prime. This applies even to farm eggs which are no longer allowed to be sold straight from the farm. Look for the lion quality stamp (on 75 per cent of all eggs sold) which guarantees that the eggs come from hens vaccinated against salmonella, have been laid in the UK and are produced to the highest food safety and standards. All of these eggs carry a best before date.

❧ **Size** Do remember that 'value' or 'economy' eggs may be ungraded and of different sizes, so, for best results, buy eggs marked as 'medium' and 'large'. If you do use economy eggs, make sure to note the sizes you are using and try to even out the quantity by, say, using 1 large and 2 small eggs instead of 3 medium-sized ones.

- **Types** There are many types of eggs sold and it really is a question of personal preference which ones are chosen. All offer the same nutritional benefits. More than half of the eggs sold in the UK are from caged hens. These are the cheapest eggs, from hens who have been fed on a manufactured mixed diet. Barn eggs are from hens kept in barns who are free to roam within the barn. However, their diet is similar to caged hens and the barns may be overcrowded.

- **Free-range** It is commonly thought that free-range eggs are from hens that lead a much more natural life and are fed natural foods. This, however, is not always the case and in some instances they may still live in a crowded environment and be fed the same foods as caged and barn hens. However, it is good that the production of eggs from caged hens is steadily decreasing in favour of free-range eggs – with more and more shops selling only free-range.

- **Four-grain and Organic** Four-grain eggs are from hens that have been fed on grain and no preventative medicines have been included in their diet. Organic eggs are from hens that live in a flock, whose beaks are not clipped and who are completely free to roam. Obviously, these eggs are much more expensive than the others.

- **Storage** Store eggs in the refrigerator with the round end uppermost (as packed in the egg boxes). Allow to come to room temperature before using. Do remember, raw or semi-cooked eggs should not be given to babies, toddlers, pregnant women, the elderly and those suffering from a recurring illness.

- **Separating Eggs** When separating eggs (that is, separating the white from the yolk), crack an egg in half lightly and cleanly over a bowl, being careful not to break the yolk and keeping the yolk in the shell. Then tip the yolk backwards and forwards between the two shell halves, allowing as much of the white as possible to spill out into the bowl. Keep or discard the yolk and/or the white as needed. Make sure that you do not get any yolk in your whites as this will prevent successful whisking of the whites. It takes practice!

Essential Ingredients

Sugar

Sugar not only offers taste to baking but also adds texture and volume to the mixture. It is generally accepted that caster sugar is best for sponge cakes, puddings and meringues. Its fine granules disperse evenly when creaming or whisking. Granulated sugar is used for more general cooking, such as stewing fruit, whereas demerara sugar, with its toffee taste and crunchy texture, is good for sticky puddings and cakes such as flapjacks. For rich fruit cakes, Christmas puddings and cakes, use the muscovado sugars (soft dark brown or golden brown), which give a rich intense molasses or treacle flavour.

- ∾ **Icing sugar** is used primarily for icings and can be used in meringues and in fruit sauces when the sugar needs to dissolve quickly.

- ∾ **For a different flavour**, try flavouring your own sugar, for example with vanilla. Place a vanilla pod in a screw-top jar, fill with caster sugar, screw down the lid and leave for 2–3 weeks before using. Top up with more sugar after use. You can also use thinly pared lemon or orange zest in the same manner.

- ∾ **Reducing Sugar Intake** If trying to reduce sugar intake, then use the unrefined varieties, such as golden granulated, golden caster, unrefined demerara and the muscovado sugars. All of these are a little sweeter than their refined counterparts, so less is required. Alternatively, clear honey or fructose (fruit sugar) can reduce sugar intake as they have similar calories to sugar, but are twice as sweet. Also, they have a slow release, so their effect lasts longer. Dried fruits can also be included in the diet to top up sugar intake.

Yeast

There is something very comforting about the aroma of freshly baked bread and the taste is far different and superior to commercially made bread. Bread-making is regarded by some as being a time-consuming process but, with the advent of fast-acting yeast, this no longer applies. There are three types of yeast available: fresh yeast, granular dried yeast (which is available in tins) and fast-action yeast powder, which comes in separate sachets in packets.

∾ **Fresh** Fresh yeast is rarely sold as a block any more. Commercial baker's yeast is now sold in a liquid form and is not easily available for the general public to buy. If you do manage to find firm fresh yeast, it should be bought in small quantities (although it freezes well); it has a putty-like colour and texture with a slight wine smell. It should be creamed with a little sugar and some warm liquid before being added to the flour. If you have liquid yeast, just sprinkle on sugar and stir. However, dried yeast is much easier to find and use.

∾ **Dried** Dried yeast can be stored for up to six months and comes in small hard granules. It should be sprinkled onto lukewarm liquid with a little sugar, then left to stand, normally between 15–20 minutes, until the mixture froths. When replacing fresh yeast with dried yeast, use 1 tablespoon dried yeast for 25 g/1 oz fresh yeast.

∾ **Fast-action** Quick-acting yeast – generally now sold as 'fast-action yeast' and also known formerly as 'easy-blend' – cuts down the time of bread-making as it eliminates the need for proving the bread twice and can be added straight to the flour without it needing to be activated. When using quick-acting yeast instead of dried yeast, follow recipes that specifically use fast-action yeast. When using yeast, the most important thing to remember is that yeast is a living plant and needs food, water and warmth to work.

Essential Ingredients

EQUIPMENT

Nowadays, you can get lost in the cookware sections of some of the larger stores – they really are a cook's paradise with gadgets, cooking tools and state-of-the-art electronic blenders, mixers and liquidisers. A few well-picked, high-quality utensils and pieces of equipment will be frequently used and will therefore be a much wiser buy than cheaper gadgets.

Cooking equipment not only assists in the kitchen, but can make all the difference between success and failure. Take the humble cake tin: although a very basic piece of cooking equipment, it plays an essential role in baking. Using the incorrect size can mean disaster – a tin that is too large, for example, will spread the mixture too thinly and the result will be a flat, limp-looking cake. On the other hand, cramming the mixture into a tin which is too small will result in the mixture rising up and out of the tin.

Baking Tins & Utensils

To ensure successful baking, it is worth investing in a selection of high-quality tins, which, if looked after properly, should last for many years. Choose heavy-duty metal tins that will not buckle or the new flexible silicone tins – these are easy to turn out, most need very little greasing for a perfect shape and they also wash and dry easily. Follow the manufacturer's instructions when first using and ensure that the tins are thoroughly washed and dried after use and before putting away.

- **Sandwich Tins** Perhaps the most useful of tins for baking are sandwich tins, ideal for classics such as Victoria sponge, Genoese cake and coffee and walnut cake. You will need two tins, normally 18 cm/7 inches or 20.5 cm/8 inches in diameter and about 5–7.5 cm/2–3 inches deep. They are often nonstick.

- **Deep Cake Tins** With deep cake tins, it is personal choice whether you buy round or square tins and they vary in size from 12.5–35.5 cm/5–14 inches (a useful size is 20.5 cm/8 inches), with a depth of between 12.5–15 cm/5–6 inches. A deep cake tin, for everyday fruit or Madeira cake, is a must.

- **Loaf Tins** Loaf tins are used for bread, fruit or tea breads and terrines and normally come in two sizes: 450 g/1 lb and 900 g/2 lb.

- **Baking Sheets and Trays** Good baking sheets and trays are a must for all cooks. Dishes that are too hot to handle such as apple pies should be placed directly onto a baking sheet. Meringues, biscuits and cookies are cooked on the sheet. The difference between baking sheets and baking trays – or specific Swiss-roll tins – is that they have sides all around, whereas a sheet only has one raised side, or none.

- **Other Tins and Dishes** Square or oblong shallow baking tins are also very useful for making traybakes, fudge brownies, flapjacks and shortbread. Then there are patty tins, which are ideal for making small buns, jam tarts or mince pies; and individual Yorkshire pudding tins, muffin tins or flan tins. They are available in a variety of sizes.

There are plenty of other tins to choose from, ranging from themed tins, such as Christmas tree shapes, numbers from 1–9 and tins shaped as petals, to ring-mould tins (tins with a hole in the centre) and springform tins, where the sides release after cooking, allowing the finished cake to be removed easily.

A selection of different-sized roasting tins (deep baking trays) are also a worthwhile investment as they can double up as a bain-marie, or for cooking larger quantities of cakes such as

Equipment

gingerbread. A few different tins and dishes are required if baking crumbles, soufflés and pies. Ramekin dishes and small pudding basins can be used for a variety of different recipes, as can small tartlet tins and dariole moulds.

∾ Cooling Racks Another piece of equipment which is worth having is a wire cooling rack. It is essential when baking to allow biscuits and cakes to cool (in their tins and/or after being removed from their tins), and a wire rack protects your kitchen surfaces from the heat as well as allowing air to circulate around the goodies, speeding cooling and preventing soggy bottoms.

∾ Rolling Pin When purchasing your implements for baking, perhaps the rolling pin is one of the most important. Ideally, it should be long and thin, and heavy enough to roll the pastry out easily but not too heavy that it is uncomfortable to use. Pastry needs to be rolled out on a flat surface and, although a lightly floured flat surface will do, a marble slab will ensure that the pastry is kept cool and ensures that the fats do not melt while being rolled. This helps to keep the pastry light, crisp and flaky rather than heavy and stodgy, which happens if the fat melts before being baked.

∾ Other Tools Other useful basic pastry implements are tools such as a pastry brush (which can be used to wet pastry or brush on a glaze), a pastry wheel for cutting and a sieve to remove impurities and also to sift air into the flour, encouraging the pastry or mixture to be lighter in texture.

Basic mixing cutlery is also essential, such as a wooden spoon (for mixing and creaming), a spatula (for transferring the mixture from the mixing bowl to the baking tins and spreading the mixture once it is in the tins) and a palette knife (to ease cakes and breads out of their tins before placing them on the wire racks to cool). Scales and measuring jugs, or measuring spoons and cups, are essential for accurate measuring of both dry and wet ingredients. Three to four different sizes of mixing bowls are also very useful.

Electrical Equipment

Nowadays, help from time-saving gadgets and electrical equipment makes baking far easier and quicker. Equipment can be used for creaming, mixing, beating, whisking, kneading, grating and chopping. There is a wide choice of machines available, from the most basic to the very sophisticated.

❧ **Food Processors** When choosing a machine, first, decide what you need your processor to do. If you are a novice to baking, it may be a waste to start with a machine which offers a wide range of implements and functions. This can be off-putting and result in not using the machine to its fullest. In general, while styling and product design play a role in the price, the more you pay, the larger the machine will be with a bigger bowl capacity and many more gadgets attached. Nowadays, you can chop, shred, slice, chip, blend, purée, knead, whisk and cream anything. However, just what basic features should you ensure your machine has before buying it?

When buying a food processor, look for measurements on the side of the processor bowl and machines with a removable feed tube, which allows food or liquid to be added while the motor is still running. Look out for machines that have the facility to increase the capacity of the bowl (ideal when making soup) and have a pulse button for controlled chopping. For many, storage is also an issue, so reversible discs and flex storage, or, on more advanced models, a blade storage compartment or box, can be advantageous.

Equipment

It is also worth thinking about machines that offer optional extras that can be bought as your cooking requirements change. Mini chopping bowls are available for those wanting to chop small quantities of food. If time is an issue, dishwasher-friendly attachments may be vital. Citrus presses, liquidisers and whisks may all be useful attachments for the individual cook.

∞ Blenders Blenders often come as attachments to food processors and are generally used for liquidising and puréeing foods. There are two main types of blender. The first is known as a goblet blender. The blades of this blender are at the bottom of the goblet with measurements up the sides. The second blender is portable. It is hand-held and should be placed in a bowl to blend.

∞ Food Mixers These are ideally suited to mixing cakes and kneading dough, either as a table-top mixer or a hand-held mixer. Both are extremely useful and based on the same principle of mixing or whisking in an open bowl to allow more air to get to the mixture and therefore give a lighter texture.

∞ The table-top mixers are freestanding and are capable of dealing with fairly large quantities of mixture. They are robust machines, capable of easily dealing with kneading dough and heavy cake mixing as well as whipping cream, whisking egg whites or making one-stage cakes. These mixers also offer a wide range of attachments, from liquidisers and juicers, to can openers and mincers.

∞ Hand-held mixers are smaller than freestanding mixers and often come with their own bowl and stand from which they can be lifted off and used as hand-held devices. They have a motorised head with detachable twin whisks. These mixers are particularly versatile as they do not need a specific bowl in which to whisk. Any suitable mixing bowl can be used.

BASIC TECHNIQUES

There is no mystery to successful baking; it really is easy, providing you follow a few simple rules and guidelines. First, read the recipe right through before commencing. There is nothing more annoying than getting to the middle of a recipe and discovering that you are minus one or two of the ingredients. Until you are confident, follow a recipe; do not try a short cut, otherwise you may find that you have left out a vital step which means that the recipe really cannot work. Most of all, have patience, baking is easy – if you can read, you can bake.

Working with Pastry

Pastry dough needs to be kept as cool as possible throughout. Cool hands help, but are not essential. Use cold or iced water, but not too much, as pastry does not need to be wet. Make sure that your fat is not runny or melted but firm (this is why block fat is the best). Avoid using too much flour when rolling out as this alters the proportions, and also avoid handling the dough too much. Chill pastry, wrapped in foil or a plastic bag, for 30 minutes after making the dough. Roll in one direction, as this helps to ensure that the pastry does not shrink. Allow the pastry to rest, preferably in the refrigerator, after rolling. If you follow these guidelines but still your pastry is not as good as you would like it to be, then make in a processor instead.

Lining a Flan Dish/Tart Pan

It is important to choose the right tin or dish to bake with. You will often find that a loose-bottomed metal flan tin/tart pan is the best option, as it conducts heat more efficiently and evenly than a ceramic dish. It also has the added advantage of a removable base, which makes the transfer of the final flan or tart a much simpler process; it simply lifts out, keeping the pastry intact.

1. Roll the pastry dough out on a lightly floured surface, ensuring that it is a few inches larger than the flan tin.

2. Wrap the pastry round the rolling pin, lift and place in the tin. Carefully ease the pastry into the base and sides of the tin, ensuring that there are no gaps or tears in the pastry. Allow to rest for a few minutes.

3. Trim the edge either with a sharp knife or by rolling a rolling pin across the top of the flan tin. Prick the pastry with the tines of a fork to prevent it from rising up during baking and chill before baking.

Baking Blind

The term 'baking blind' means cooking the pastry case/pie crust without the filling, resulting in a crisp pastry shell that is either partially or fully cooked, depending on whether the filling needs any cooking. Pastry shells can be prepared ahead of time, as they last for several days if stored correctly in an airtight container, or longer if frozen.

1. Line a tin or dish with the prepared pastry dough and allow to rest in the refrigerator for 30 minutes. This will help to minimize shrinkage while it is being cooked.

2. Remove from the refrigerator and lightly prick the base all over with a fork (unless the filling is runny). Line the case with a large square of greaseproof paper, big enough to cover both the base and sides of the pastry case.

3. Fill with ceramic baking beans/pie weights, dried beans or rice. Place on a baking sheet and bake in a preheated oven, generally at 200˚C/400˚F/Gas Mark 6, remembering that ovens can take at least 15 minutes to reach this heat (unless they are fan/convection ovens, see page 22). Cook for 10–12 minutes, then remove from the oven, discarding the paper and beans.

4. Return to the oven and continue to cook for a further 5–10 minutes, depending on whether the filling needs cooking. Normally, unless otherwise stated, individual pastry tartlet cases also benefit from baking blind.

Covering a Pie with a Pastry Lid

1. Roll out the pastry dough until it is about 5 cm/2 inches larger than the circumference of the dish.

2. Cut a 2.5 cm/1 inch strip from around the outside of the pastry and then moisten the edge of the pie dish you are using. Place the strip on the edge of the dish and brush with water or beaten egg.

3. Generously fill the pie dish until the surface is slightly rounded. Using the rolling pin, lift the remaining pastry and cover the pie dish. Press together, then seal.

4. Using a sharp knife, trim off any excess pastry from around the edges, then brush the top with beaten egg. Try to avoid brushing the edges of the pastry, especially puff pastry, as this prevents the pastry rising evenly. Before placing in the oven, make a small hole in the centre of the pie to allow the steam to escape.

Decorative Pie Edges

The edges of a pie can be decorated by pressing the back of a fork around the edge or, instead, crimp by pinching the edge of the crust, holding the thumb and index finger of one hand against the edge while gently pushing with the index finger of your other hand. Other ways of finishing the pie are to knock up (achieved by gently pressing your index finger down onto the rim and, at the same time, tapping a knife horizontally along the edge, giving it a flaky appearance), or fluting the edges by pressing your thumb down on the edge of the pastry while gently drawing back an all-purpose knife about 1 cm/¹/₂ inch and repeating around the rim. Experiment by putting leaves and berries made out of leftover pastry to finish off the pie, then brush the top of the pie with beaten egg.

Greasing and Lining Cake Tins

Most tins/pans will at least need oiling or greasing with butter (butter is better, as oil runs off lining paper). If a recipe states that the tin needs lining, do not be tempted to ignore this. Rich fruit cakes and other cakes that take a long time to cook benefit from the tin being lined so that the edges and base do not burn or dry out. Greaseproof/waxed paper or baking parchment is ideal for this. It is a good idea to have the paper at least double thickness, or preferably 3–4 thicknesses. Sponge cakes and other cakes that are cooked in 30 minutes or less are also better if the bases are lined, as it is far easier to remove them from the tin. Steamed puddings usually need only a disc of greaseproof paper at the bottom of the dish so that it will turn out easily. The best way to line a round or square tin is as follows:

1. Lightly draw around the base and then cut just inside the markings, making it easy to sit in the tin.

2. Next, lightly grease the paper (with butter) so that it will easily peel away from the cake.

3. If the sides of the tin also need to be lined, then cut a strip of paper long enough for the tin. This can be measured by wrapping a piece of string around the rim of the tin.

4. Once again, lightly grease the paper, push against the tin and grease once more, as this will hold the paper to the sides of the tin.

Hints for Successful Baking

Measurements
Ensure that the ingredients are accurately measured. A cake that has too much flour or insufficient egg will be dry and crumbly. Take care when measuring the raising/leavening agent if used, as too much will mean that the cake will rise too quickly and then sink, whilst not enough means the cake will not rise adequately.

Oven Temperature
Ensure that the oven is preheated to the correct temperature; it can take 10 minutes to reach up to 190°C/375°F/Gas Mark 5, and 15 minutes for above that – but ovens vary. You may find that an oven thermometer is a good investment. Cakes are best if cooked in the centre of the preheated oven. Do try to avoid the temptation of opening the oven door at the beginning of cooking, as a draught of

cool air can make the cake sink. Important: if using a fan/convection oven, then refer to the manufacturer's instructions, as they normally cook 10–20°C/50–68°F hotter than conventional ovens and often do not need preheating. As a general rule, preheat your fan oven to 20 per cent lower than is stated for a non-fan oven – this usually works out at 20°C/68°F lower.

Testing to See When a Cake is Cooked

Check that the cake is thoroughly cooked by removing from the oven and inserting a clean skewer into the cake. Leave for 30 seconds and remove. If the skewer is completely clean, then the cake is cooked; if there is a little mixture left on the skewer, then return to the oven for a few minutes.

Problems

Other problems that you may encounter while baking are insufficient creaming of the fat and sugar or a curdled creamed mixture (which will result in a densely textured and often fairly solid cake). Flour that has not been folded in carefully enough or has not been mixed with enough raising agent may also result in a heavy consistency. It is important to ensure that the correct tin size is used, as you may end up either with a flat, hard cake or one which has spilled over the edge of the tin/pan. Another tip to be aware of when cooking with fruit is that, if the consistency is too soft, the cake will not be able to support the fruit.

Cooling and Storing

Finally, when you take your cake out of the oven, unless the recipe states that it should be left in the tin until cold, leave for a few minutes to settle, then loosen the edges and turn out onto a wire rack to cool. Cakes which are left in the tin for too long will develop a damp, soggy base.

When storing, make sure the cake is completely cold before placing it into an airtight container. Generally, biscuits/cookies and cakes will keep for about 5 days in an airtight container. However, if a cake uses fresh cream, cream cheese frosting or other fresh ingredients such as fruit, it will only last for 1–2 days kept refrigerated (note: do not refrigerate cakes covered with sugarpaste/rolled fondant icing). Cakes with buttercream and similar icings will keep for 2–3 days in a cool place. Light fruit cakes such as Dundee will store for about a week and rich fruit cakes such as Christmas Cake will keep for up to 3 months if fortified with alcohol and wrapped tightly in foil.

Basic Techniques

BASIC RECIPES: PASTRY

Pastry

Shortcrust Pastry
Makes 225 g/8 oz

225 g/8 oz plain white flour
pinch salt
50 g/2 oz white vegetable fat or lard
50 g/2 oz butter or block margarine

Sift the flour and salt into a mixing bowl. Cut the fats into small pieces and add to the bowl. Rub the fats into the flour using your fingertips until the mixture resembles fine breadcrumbs. Add 1–2 tablespoons of cold water and, using a knife or your hands if easier, mix to form a soft, pliable dough. Knead gently on a lightly floured surface until smooth and free from cracks, then wrap and chill for 30 minutes before rolling out on a lightly floured surface. Use as required. Cook in a preheated hot oven (200°C/400°F/ Gas Mark 6).

Sweet Shortcrust Pastry (Pâte Sucrée)
Makes 225 g/8 oz

225 g/8 oz plain white flour
150 g/5 oz unsalted butter, softened
2 tbsp caster sugar
1 egg yolk

Sift the flour into a mixing bowl, cut the butter into small pieces, add to the bowl and rub into the flour. Stir in the sugar, then mix to form a pliable dough with the egg yolk and about 1 tablespoon of cold water. Wrap, chill for at least 30 minutes or until firm and use as required.

Chocolate Variation

To make sweet chocolate shortcrust pastry, simply sift in 1 tablespoon cocoa powder with the flour after the butter has been rubbed in.

Cheese Pastry

Follow the recipe for sweet shortcrust pastry, but omit the sugar and add 1 teaspoon dried mustard powder and 50 g/2 oz mature grated Cheddar cheese.

Rough Puff Pastry
Makes 225 g/8 oz

225 g/8 oz plain flour
pinch salt
150 g/5 oz butter, block margarine or lard
squeeze lemon juice

Sift the flour and salt together in a mixing bowl. Cut up the fat and add to the bowl. Add the lemon juice and 6–7 tablespoons of cold water. Mix with a fork until it is a fairly stiff mixture.

Turn out onto a lightly floured surface. Roll into an oblong. Fold the bottom third up to the centre, bring the top third down to the centre. Gently press the edges together.

Give the pastry a half turn, roll the pastry out again into an oblong. Repeat the folding, turning and rolling at least four times. Wrap. Leave to rest in a cool place for at least 30 minutes. Cook as directed by your recipe, in a preheated oven at 220°C/425°F/Gas Mark 7.

Quick Flaky Pastry

125 g/4 oz butter
175 g/6 oz plain flour
pinch salt

Place the butter in the freezer for 30 minutes. Sift the flour and salt into a large bowl. Remove the butter from the freezer and grate using the coarse side of a grater, dipping the butter in the flour every now and again as it makes it easier to grate.

Mix the butter into the flour, using a knife, making sure all the butter is coated thoroughly with flour. Add 2 tablespoons cold water and continue to mix, bringing the mixture together. Use your hands to complete the mixing. Add a little more water if needed to leave a clean bowl. Place the pastry in a polythene bag and chill in the refrigerator for 30 minutes. Cook as directed by your recipe, in a preheated oven at 200°C/400°F/Gas Mark 6.

Choux Pastry

Makes 225 g/8 oz

50 g/2 oz butter
75 g/3 oz plain flour
pinch salt
2 eggs, beaten

FRESH BREAD
Bakery
CAKES & PASTRIES

Place the butter and 150 ml/5 fl oz water in a heavy-based saucepan. Heat gently, stirring until the butter has melted, and bring to the boil. Draw off the heat and add the flour and salt all at once.

Beat with a wooden spoon until the mixture forms a ball in the centre. Cool for 5 minutes. Gradually add the eggs, beating well after each addition until a stiff mixture is formed. Either place in a piping bag fitted with a large nozzle, or shape using two spoons.

Place on a greased baking sheet and bake in a preheated oven at 200°C/400°F/Gas Mark 6 for 15–25 minutes, depending on size. Remove and make a small slit in the side, then return to the oven and cook for a further 5 minutes. Remove and cool before filling.

Hot Water Crust Pastry
Makes 450 g/1 lb

450 g/1 lb plain flour
1 tsp salt
125 g/4 oz lard or white vegetable fat
150 ml/¹/₄ pt milk and water, mixed

Sift the flour and salt together and reserve. Heat the lard or white vegetable fat until melted. Bring to the boil. Pour immediately into the flour along with some of the milk and water and, using a wooden spoon, mix together and beat until the mixture comes together and forms a ball, using more milk and water as needed.

When cool enough to handle, knead lightly until smooth and pliable. Use as required, covering the dough with a clean cloth before use. Bake in a preheated oven at 220°C/425°F/Gas Mark 7, or as directed.

BASIC RECIPES: BATTERS

Batters

Pouring Batter for Yorkshire Puddings and Pancakes

125 g/4 oz plain white flour
pinch salt
2 medium/large eggs
300 ml/½ pint whole milk and water, mixed
1 tbsp vegetable oil, for baking the Yorkshire puddings

1. Sift the flour and salt into a mixing bowl and make a well in the centre.

2. Drop the eggs into the well with a little milk.

3. Beat the eggs into the flour, gradually drawing the flour in from the sides of the bowl.

4. Once half the milk has been added, beat well until smooth and free from lumps. Stir in the remaining milk and leave to stand for 30 minutes. Stir before using.

This batter can be used for pancakes and, if liked, 2 tbsp caster/superfine sugar can be added.

Using pouring batter to make Yorkshire puddings

1. Heat 1 tablespoon oil in a roasting tin/pan or individual Yorkshire pudding tins/pans in an oven preheated to 220°C/425°F/Gas Mark 7.

2. When the oil is almost smoking, stir the batter, then pour it into the hot oil.

3. Cook for 30–40 minutes for a large pudding and 18–20 minutes for individual puddings.

Coating Batter for Fritters

125 g/4 oz plain flour
pinch salt
1 tbsp sunflower
150 ml/¼ pint cup water
2 medium/large egg whites

1. Sift the flour and salt into a mixing bowl and make a well in the centre.

2. Add the oil and half the water and beat until smooth and free from lumps.

3. Gradually beat in the remaining water.

4. Just before using, whisk the egg whites until stiff, then stir into the batter and use immediately to coat your fritters.

BASIC RECIPES: MERINGUES

Meringues

Meringue is made from egg whites and caster/superfine sugar.
As a general rule, allow 1 medium/large egg white to
50 g/2 oz caster sugar.
If liked, add a pinch of salt at the start of whisking.

Making Meringue

1. Place the egg whites in a clean mixing bowl (any grease
    in the bowl will prevent the egg white from whisking).

2. Use a balloon or wire whisk if whisking by hand, or an
    electric mixer fitted with a balloon whisk if not.

3. Whisk the egg whites until stiff. To test if they are stiff
    enough, turn the bowl upside down – if the egg white
    does not move, it is ready.

4. Slowly add half the sugar, 1 teaspoon at a time,
    whisking well after each addition.

5. Once half the sugar has been added, add the
    remaining sugar and gently stir it in with a metal
    spoon. Take care not to overmix.

6. Spoon the meringue onto a baking sheet lined with nonstick baking parchment. Shape the meringue according to preference or the recipe – such as in a round 'case' – and bake in a preheated oven at 150°C/300°F/Gas Mark 2 for 1¹/₂ hours, or until set and firm to the touch.

7. Once cooked, ideally leave the meringue in the oven for a while to cool slowly and dry out properly. Remove from the oven and leave until fully cold before using or storing in an airtight container.

Whipped Cream
(to accompany the meringues)

Whipping cream, double cream or a combination of single cream and double cream will all whip. For the combination option, use one third single cream and two thirds double cream. Whipped cream is ideal for using in soufflés, mousses and other cream desserts.

1. Place the cream in a mixing bowl and use a balloon whisk, wire whisk or electric mixer fitted with the balloon whisk attachment. Place the bowl on a damp cloth if whipping by hand.

2. Whip until thickened and soft peaks are formed – this is when the whisk, if dragged gently through the cream and lifted out, leaves soft peaks in the cream.

3. For piping/decorating and to use as a filling, whip for a little longer until the cream is slightly stiffer. If using only double cream, take care that you do not overwhip, as it will curdle.

BASIC RECIPES: ICINGS

Cream Cheese Frosting

Covers a 20 cm/8 inch round cake or 12 small cakes

50 g/2 oz unsalted butter, softened
300 g/11 oz icing sugar, sifted
flavouring of choice
food colourings
125 g/4 oz full-fat cream cheese

Beat the butter and icing sugar together until light and fluffy. Add flavourings and colourings of choice and beat again. Add the cream cheese and whisk until light and fluffy. Do not over-beat, however, as the mixture can become runny.

Basic Buttercream Frosting

Covers a 20 cm/8 inch round cake or 12 small cakes

150 g/5 oz unsalted butter, softened
225 g/8 oz icing sugar, sifted
2 tbsp hot milk or water
1 tsp vanilla extract
food colourings of choice

FAMILY BAKERS
★ ★ ★
ESTD 1993
BREADS & PASTRIES

Beat the butter until light and fluffy, then beat in the sifted icing sugar and hot milk or water in two batches. Add the vanilla extract and any food colourings. Store chilled for up to 2 days in a lidded container.

Variations
Omit the vanilla extract and instead:

- ∿ Coffee Blend 2 tsp coffee extract with the milk.

- ∿ Chocolate Blend 2 tbsp cocoa powder to a paste with 2 tbsp boiling water and use instead of the hot milk or water.

- ∿ Citrus Add the finely grated zest of 1 small orange plus 1 tbsp orange juice or the finely grated zest of 1 lemon or lime and 2 tsp fresh lemon or lime juice instead of the milk or water.

Chocolate Fudge Icing

Covers a 20 cm/8 inch round cake or 12 small cakes

125 g/4 oz dark chocolate, broken into pieces
50 g/2 oz unsalted butter
1 medium egg, beaten
175 g/6 oz natural icing sugar, sifted
1/2 tsp vanilla extract

Place the chocolate and butter in a bowl over a pan of hot water and stir until melted. Remove from the heat and whisk in the egg with the icing sugar and vanilla. Whisk until smooth and glossy, then use immediately or leave to cool and thicken for a spreading consistency.

Basic Recipes: Icings

Royal Icing

Makes 500 g/1 lb 2 oz to cover a 20cm/8 inch round cake or 12 deep muffins

2 medium egg whites
500 g/1 lb 2 oz icing sugar, sifted
2 tsp lemon juice

Put the egg whites in a large bowl and whisk lightly with a fork to break up the whites until foamy. Sift in half the icing sugar with the lemon juice and beat well with an electric mixer for 4 minutes or by hand with a wooden spoon for about 10 minutes until smooth. Gradually sift in the remaining icing sugar and beat again until thick, smooth and brilliant white and the icing forms soft peaks when flicked up with a spoon. Keep the royal icing covered with a clean damp cloth until you are ready to use it, or store in the refrigerator in a tightly lidded plastic container until needed. If making royal icing ahead of time to use later, beat it again before use to remove any air bubbles that may have formed in the mixture.

Tip For a softer royal icing that will not set too hard, beat 1 tsp of glycerine into the mixture.

Glacé Icing

Covers the top of a 20cm/8 inch round cake or 12 small cakes

225 g/8 oz icing sugar
few drops lemon juice or vanilla
or almond extract
2–3 tbsp boiling water
liquid food colouring

Sift the icing sugar into a bowl and add the chosen flavouring. Gradually stir in enough water to mix to a consistency of thick cream. Beat with a wooden spoon until the icing is thick enough to coat the back of the spoon. Add colouring if liked and use at once, as the icing will begin to form a skin.

Variations

- **Citrus** Replace the water with freshly squeezed, strained orange or lemon juice.

- **Chocolate** Sift 2 tsp cocoa powder into the icing sugar.

- **Coffee** Dissolve 1 tsp coffee granules in 1 tbsp of the hot water, cool; or add 1 tsp liquid coffee extract.

Apricot Glaze

Makes 450 g/1 lb to cover two 20cm/8 inch round cakes or 24 small cakes

450 g/1 lb apricot jam
3 tbsp water
1 tsp lemon juice

Place the jam, water and juice in a heavy-based saucepan and heat gently, stirring, until soft and melted. Boil rapidly for 1 minute, then press through a fine sieve with the back of a wooden spoon. Discard the pieces of fruit. Use immediately for glazing or sticking on almond paste, or pour into a clean jar or plastic lidded container and store in the refrigerator for up to 3 months.

Basic Recipes: Icings

Almond Pa/te

Cakes

Makes 450 g/1 lb to cover two 20cm/8 inch
round cakes or 24 small cakes

125 g/4 oz icing sugar, sifted
125 g/4 oz caster sugar
225 g/8 oz ground almonds
1 medium egg
1 tsp lemon juice

Stir the sugars and ground almonds together in a bowl.
Whisk the egg and lemon juice together and mix into the dry
ingredients. Knead until the paste is smooth. Wrap tightly in clingfilm
or foil to keep airtight and store in the refrigerator until needed. The
paste can be made 2–3 days ahead of time, but after that it will start
to dry out and become difficult to handle. To use the almond paste,
knead on a surface lightly dusted with icing sugar until soft and
pliable. Brush the top of each cake with apricot glaze. Roll out the
almond paste and cut out discs large enough to cover the tops of
the cakes. Press onto the cakes.

Su/arpa/te Icing

Makes 350 g/12 oz to cover a 20cm/8 inch round cake
or12 small cakes, or use for decorations

1 medium egg white
1 tbsp liquid glucose
350 g/12 oz icing sugar, sifted

Place the egg white and liquid glucose in a large mixing bowl and stir together with a fork, breaking up the egg white. Add the icing sugar gradually, mixing in with a palette knife until the mixture binds together and forms a ball.

Turn the ball of icing out onto a clean surface dusted with icing sugar and knead for 5 minutes until soft but firm enough to roll out. If the icing is too soft, knead in a little more icing sugar until the mixture is pliable.

To colour, knead in paste food colouring. Do not use liquid food colouring as this is not suitable and will make the sugarpaste go limp.

To use, roll out thinly on a clean surface dusted with icing sugar and cut out a disc large enough to cover the top of each cake.

Brush the almond paste (if using as a layer underneath the sugarpaste disc) with a little cold boiled water or a clear spirit such as Kirsch, then press onto the cake, then press the sugarpaste on top of the almond paste topping. Alternatively, coat the cakes with a little buttercream and place the sugarpaste disc on top and press down.

To mould, knead lightly and roll out thinly on a surface dusted with icing sugar. Use cutters or templates to make flat shapes, then mould into 3D shapes with your fingertips and leave to dry out for 24 hours in egg boxes lined with clingfilm.

Basic Recipes: Icings

CULINARY TERMS EXPLAINED

*a*t a glance, here are some of the key terms you will come across when baking. Some we may have discussed already, some may be new to you.

- ❧ Baking parchment Sometimes called 'silicone-coated paper', 'baking parchment' or 'nonstick baking paper'. Used for wrapping food to be cooked (*en papillote*) and for lining cake tins to prevent sticking. As it is sold as 'nonstick', this in theory avoids the need to grease or oil the paper.

- ❧ Greaseproof paper Paper that tends to be relatively nonstick and which is used to line tins for cakes and puddings, but it is advisable to lightly grease this paper to prevent sticking. It is ideal for wrapping food such as packed lunches or fatty foods. Today, greaseproof paper and baking parchment are often able to be used in the same way – check the packaging.

- ❧ En papillote A French term used to describe food which is baked, but is wrapped in baking parchment before cooking. This works well with fish as the aroma from the different herbs or spices and the fish are contained during cooking and not released until the paper parcel is opened.

- ❧ Rice paper This edible paper is made from the pith of a Chinese tree and can be used as a base on which to bake delicate or sticky cakes and biscuits such as almond macaroons.

- **Baking blind** The method often used for cooking the pastry case of flans and tarts before the filling is added. After lining the tin with the uncooked pastry, it is then covered with a sheet of greaseproof paper or baking parchment and weighed down with either ceramic baking beans, dried beans or rice and is baked in the oven as directed in the recipe.

- **Baking powder** A raising agent for breads and cakes which works by producing carbon dioxide as a consequence of a reaction caused by the acid and alkali ingredients which expand during the baking process.

- **Bicarbonate of soda** This alkali powder acts as a raising agent in baking when combined with an acid or acid liquid (cream of tartar, lemon juice, yogurt, buttermilk, cocoa or vinegar, for example).

- **Cream of tartar** An acid raising agent (potassium hydrogen tartrate) often present in both self-raising flour and baking powder. Activates the alkali component of baking powder.

- **Fermenting** A term used during bread-, beer- or wine-making to note the chemical change brought about through the use of a fermenting or leavening agent, such as yeast.

- **Unleavened** Often refers to bread which does not use a raising agent and is therefore flat, such as Indian naan bread.

- **Cornflour** Used to thicken consistency and can also be used in meringue-making to prevent the meringue becoming hard and brittle and to enhance its chewiness.

- **Curdling** When the milk separates from a sauce through acidity or excessive heat. This can also happen to creamed cake mixtures that have separated due to the eggs being too cold or added too quickly.

⌒ **Sifting** The shaking of dry ingredients (primarily flour) through a metal or nylon sieve to remove lumps and impurities, and to add air.

⌒ **Binding** Adding liquid or egg to bring a dry mixture together. Normally, this entails using a fork, spoon or your fingertips.

⌒ **Blending** When two or more ingredients are thoroughly mixed together.

⌒ **Creaming** The method by which fat and sugar are beaten together until lighter in colour and fluffy. By creaming the fat in cake mixtures, air is incorporated into the fairly high fat content. It thus lightens the texture of cakes and puddings.

⌒ **Folding** A method of combining creamed fat and sugar with flour in cake and pudding mixes, by mixing with a large metal spoon, either by cutting and folding, or by doing a figure-of-eight in order to maintain a light texture.

⌒ **Rubbing in** The method of combining fat with flour by rubbing them together using your hands. For crumble toppings, shortcrust pastry, biscuits and scones.

⌒ **Beating** The method by which air is introduced into a mixture using a fork, wooden spoon, whisk or electric mixer. Beating is also used as a method to soften ingredients.

⌒ **Whipping/whisking** The term given to incorporating air rapidly into a mixture (either through using a manual whisk or an electric whisk).

⌒ **Dropping consistency** The consistency to which a cake or pudding mixture reaches before being cooked. It tends to be fairly soft (but not runny) and should drop off a spoon in around 5 seconds when tapped lightly on the side of a bowl.

∞ **Grinding** Reducing hard ingredients, such as nuts, to crumbs, normally by the use of a grinder or a pestle and mortar.

∞ **Blender** An electric machine with rotating blades used mainly with soft and wet ingredients to purée and liquidise, although it can grind dry ingredients such as nuts and breadcrumbs.

∞ **Knead** The process of stretching, pummelling and working dough in order to strengthen the gluten in the flour and making the dough more elastic, thus giving a good rise. Also applies to pastry-making; the dough is kneaded on a lightly floured surface to give a smooth and elastic pastry, making it easier to roll and ensuring an even texture after baking. In both cases, the outside of the dough is drawn into the centre.

∞ **Proving** The term used in bread-making when the bread is allowed to rise a second time after it has been kneaded once and then shaped before it is baked.

∞ **Knock back** The term used for a second kneading after the dough has been allowed to rise. This is done to ensure an even texture and to disperse any large pockets of air.

∞ **Crumb** The internal texture of a cake or bread as defined by the air pockets.

∞ **En croute** Used to describe food which is covered with raw pastry and then baked.

∞ **Vol-au-vent** Translated, it means to fly or float on the wind. This small and usually round or oval puff pastry case is first baked and then filled with a savoury meat, seafood or vegetable filling in a sauce.

∞ *Culinary Terms Explained*

~ Choux A type of pastry, whose uncooked dough is rather like a glossy batter, which is piped into small balls onto a baking sheet and baked until light and airy. They can then be filled with cream or savoury fillings.

~ Filo A type of pastry that is wafer thin. Three to four sheets are usually used at a time, buttered, then layered.

~ Puff pastry Probably the richest of pastries, as it is enriched with a high proportion of butter, which makes a pastry with light flaky layers. When making from the beginning, it requires the lightest of handling.

~ Brioche A sweet, spongy traditional bread eaten in France for breakfast, often served warm. Brioche is enriched with eggs and butter and has a rich but soft texture, made from a very light yeast dough, and is baked in the shape of a small cottage loaf. A delicious substitute for bread in bread and butter pudding.

~ Caramel Obtained by heating sugar on a very low heat until it turns liquid and deep brown in colour. This is used in dishes such as crème caramel, which is, in turn, baked in a bain-marie.

~ Bain-marie A French term meaning water bath. A shallow tin, often a roasting tin, is half-filled with water; smaller dishes of food are then placed in it, allowing them to cook at lower temperatures without overheating. This method is often used to cook custards and other egg dishes or to keep some dishes warm.

~ Ramekin An ovenproof earthenware dish which provides an individual serving.

∞ Cocotte Another name for a ramekin (a small, ovenproof earthenware pot used for individual portions).

∞ Dariole A small narrow mould with sloping sides used for making Madeleines. Darioles can also be used for individual steamed or baked puddings and jellies.

∞ Dusting To sprinkle lightly, often with flour, sugar or icing sugar.

∞ Dredging The sprinkling of food with a coating (generally of flour or sugar). A board may be dredged with flour before the pastry is rolled out and cakes and biscuits can be dredged with sugar or icing sugar after baking.

∞ Glacé A French term meaning glossy or iced. Glacé icing is a quick icing often used to decorate cakes and biscuits. It is made using icing sugar and warm water.

∞ Piping A way in which cakes and desserts are decorated, or the method by which choux pastry is placed onto a baking sheet. This is achieved by putting cream, icing or mixture in a nylon bag (with a nozzle attached), or an improvised piping bag made from a cone of greaseproof paper, and then slowly forcing through the nozzle and piping it onto the cake or baking sheet.

∞ Zest This can refer to the outer, coloured part of an orange, lemon or lime peel, or the very thin, long pieces of that peel. The zest contains the fruit oil, which is responsible for the citrus flavour. Normally, a zester is used to create the strips, as it removes the zest without any of the bitter white pith. Zest can also be grated on a grater into very small pieces, again taking care to only remove the very outer layer.

∞ *Culinary Terms Explained*

USEFUL CONVERSIONS

Oven Temperatures

110°C	225°F	Gas Mark 1/4	Very slow oven
120/130°C	250°F	Gas Mark 1/2	Very slow oven
140°C	275°F	Gas Mark 1	Slow oven
150°C	300°F	Gas Mark 2	Slow oven
160/170°C	325°F	Gas Mark 3	Moderate oven
180°C	350°F	Gas Mark 4	Moderate oven
190°C	375°F	Gas Mark 5	Moderately hot
200°C	400°F	Gas Mark 6	Moderately hot
220°C	425°F	Gas Mark 7	Hot oven
230°C	450°F	Gas Mark 8	Hot oven
240°C	475°F	Gas Mark 9	Very hot oven

Dry Weights

Metric	Imperial	Metric	Imperial
10 g	1/4 oz	175 g	6 oz
15 g	1/2 oz	185 g	6 1/2 oz
20 g	3/4 oz	200 g	7 oz
25 g	1 oz	225 g	8 oz
40 g	1 1/2 oz	250 g	9 oz
50 g	2 oz	275 g	10 oz
65 g	2 1/2 oz	300 g	11 oz
75 g	3 oz	325 g	11 1/2 oz
100 g	3 1/2 oz	350 g	12 oz
125 g	4 oz	375 g	13 oz
130 g	4 1/2 oz	400 g	14 oz
150 g	5 oz	425 g	15 oz
165 g	5 1/2 oz	450 g	1 lb (16 oz)

Liquid Measures

Metric	Imperial	US Cups	Quarts
2.5 ml	1/2 tsp	-	-
5 ml	1 tsp	-	-
15 ml	1 tbsp	-	-
25 ml	1 fl oz	1/8 cup	2 tbsp
50 ml	2 fl oz	1/4 cup	3–4 tbsp
65 ml	2 1/2 fl oz	1/3 cup	5 tbsp
75–85 ml	3 fl oz	1/3 cup	6 tbsp
100 ml	3 1/2 fl oz	1/3 cup	7 tbsp
120 ml	4 fl oz	1/2 cup	8 tbsp
135 ml	4 1/2 fl oz	1/2 cup	9 tbsp
150 ml	5 fl oz	1/4 pint	2/3 cup
175 ml	6 fl oz	1/3 pint	scant 3/4 cup
200 ml	7 fl oz	1/3 pint	3/4 cup
225 ml	8 fl oz	3/8 pint	1 cup
240 ml	8 fl oz	3/8 pint	1 cup
250 ml	8 fl oz	3/8 pint	1 cup
275 ml	9 fl oz	1/2 pint	1 1/8 cups
300 ml	10 fl oz	1/2 pint	1 1/4 cups
350 ml	12 fl oz	2/3 pint	1 1/2 cups
400 ml	14 fl oz	5/8 pint	1 2/3 cups
450 ml	15 fl oz	3/4 pint	1 3/4 cups
475 ml	16 fl oz	7/8 pint	2 scant cups
500 ml	18 fl oz	7/8 pint	2 cups
600 ml	20 fl oz	1 pint	2 1/2 cups
750 ml	26 fl oz	1 1/4 pints	3 1/4 cups
900 ml	-	1 1/2 pints	1 scant quart
1 litre		2 pints	1 quart
1.25 litres	-	2 1/4 pints	1 1/4 quarts
1.3 litres	-	2 1/3 pints	1 1/3 quarts
1.5 litres	-	2 1/2 pints	1 1/2 quarts
1.6 litres	-	2 3/4 pints	1 3/4 quarts
1.7 litres	-	3 pints	1 3/4 quarts
1.8 litres	-	3 3/8 pints	1 7/8 quarts
1.9 litres	-	3 1/3 pints	2 quarts
2 litres	-	3 1/2 pints	2 quarts
2.25 litres	-	4 pints	2 1/4 quarts
2.5 litres	-	4 1/4 pints	2 1/2 quarts
2.75 litres	-	5 pints	3 quarts

Temperatures

–4°F	–20°C	68°F	20°C
5°F	–15°C	77°F	25°C
14°F	–10°C	86°F	30°C
23°F	–5°C	95°F	35°C
32°F	0°C	104°F	40°C
41°F	5°C	113°F	45°C
50°F	10°C	122°F	50°C
59°F	15°C	212°F	100°C

Useful Conversions

CLASSIC CAKES & BAKES

Anyone who wants to bake cakes inevitably needs to know how to make a basic sponge – so many cakes take their cues from this. However, believe it or not, it can be tricky to create a perfectly cooked, light Victoria sponge. This section provides an easy recipe for this classic cake along with a whole range of essential standards and simple recipes, such as Carrot Cake, Fruit Cake, Coffee & Pecan Cake and even every child's favourite – Chocolate Nut Brownies.

EASY VICTORIA SPONGE

⟨⟨∞⟩⟩

Serves 8

225 g/8 oz soft margarine
225 g/8 oz caster sugar
4 medium eggs
1 tsp vanilla extract
225 g/8 oz self-raising flour
1 tsp baking powder
icing sugar, to dust

For the filling:

4 tbsp seedless raspberry jam
100 ml/3½ fl oz double cream

Preheat the oven to 180°C/350°F/Gas Mark 4. Grease two 20.5 cm/8 inch sandwich tins and line the bases with nonstick baking parchment.

Place the margarine, sugar, eggs and vanilla extract in a large bowl and sift in the flour and baking powder. Beat for about 2 minutes until smooth and blended, then divide between the tins and smooth level.

Bake for about 25 minutes until golden, well risen and the tops of the cakes spring back when lightly touched with a fingertip. Leave to cool in the tins for 2 minutes, then turn out onto a wire rack to cool. When cold, peel away the baking parchment.

When completely cold, spread one cake with jam and place on a serving plate. Whip the cream until it forms soft peaks, then spread on the underside of the other cake. Sandwich the two cakes together and sift a little icing sugar over the top.

FAT-FREE SPONGE

❧

Serves 8

3 medium eggs
175 g/6 oz caster sugar,
plus extra for dusting
125 g/4 oz self-raising flour,
plus extra for dusting

To decorate:

150 ml/¼ pint low-fat whipping
cream, or low-fat crème fraîche
or yogurt
2 tbsp lemon curd
125 g/4 oz blueberries
zest of 1 lemon, cut into long
thin strips

Preheat the oven to 190°C/375°F/Gas Mark 5. Grease two nonstick 18 cm/ 7 inch sandwich tins, line with nonstick baking parchment, then dust with a mixture of flour and caster sugar.

Put the eggs and sugar in a bowl and stand over a pan of hot water. Whisk the eggs and sugar until doubled in volume and the mixture is thick enough to leave a trail on the surface of the batter when the whisk is lifted away.

Remove the bowl from the heat and continue whisking for a further 5 minutes until the mixture is cool. Sift half the flour over the mixture and fold in lightly, using a large metal spoon. Sift in the remaining flour and fold in.

Pour the mixture into the prepared tins and tilt them to spread the mixture evenly. Bake for 15–20 minutes until well risen and firm and the cakes are beginning to shrink away from the sides of the tins. Leave to stand for 2 minutes, then turn out to cool on a wire rack.

To decorate, whip the cream, if using, and spread half the cream (or crème fraîche or yogurt) over one cake. Swirl 1 tablespoon lemon curd into the cream, crème fraîche or yogurt and scatter over half the blueberries. Place the other cake on top and swirl over the remaining cream/yogurt. Swirl over 1 tablespoon lemon curd and sprinkle with the remaining berries. Scatter the strips of lemon zest over the top.

CARROT CAKE

❦

Cuts into 8 slices

200 g/7 oz plain flour
$^1/_2$ tsp ground cinnamon
$^1/_2$ tsp freshly grated nutmeg
1 tsp baking powder
1 tsp bicarbonate of soda
150 g/5 oz dark muscovado sugar
200 ml/7 fl oz vegetable oil
3 medium eggs
225 g/8 oz carrots, peeled and
roughly grated
50 g/2 oz chopped walnuts

For the icing:

175 g/6 oz cream cheese
finely grated zest of 1 orange
1 tbsp orange juice
1 tsp vanilla extract
125 g/4 oz icing sugar

Preheat the oven to 150°C/300°F/Gas Mark 2, 10 minutes before baking. Lightly oil and line the base of a 15 cm/ 6 inch deep square cake tin with greaseproof or baking paper.

Sift the flour, spices, baking powder and bicarbonate of soda together into a large bowl. Stir in the dark muscovado sugar and mix together.

Lightly whisk the oil and eggs together, then gradually stir into the flour and sugar mixture. Stir well. Add the carrots and walnuts. Mix thoroughly, then pour into the prepared cake tin. Bake in the preheated oven for 1$^1/_4$ hours, or until light and springy to the touch and a skewer inserted into the centre of the cake comes out clean.

Remove from the oven and allow to cool in the tin for 5 minutes before turning out onto a wire rack. Reserve until cold.

To make the icing, beat together the cream cheese, orange zest, orange juice and vanilla extract. Sift the icing sugar and stir into the cream cheese mixture.

When the cake is cold, discard the lining paper, spread the cream cheese icing over the top and serve cut into squares.

BANANA CAKE

༄

Cuts into 8 slices

3 medium-sized ripe bananas
1 tsp lemon juice
150 g/5 oz soft brown sugar
75 g/3 oz butter or margarine
250 g/9 oz self-raising flour
1 tsp ground cinnamon
3 medium eggs
50 g/2 oz walnuts, chopped
1 tsp each ground cinnamon and
caster sugar, to decorate
fresh cream, to serve

Preheat the oven to 190°C/375°F/Gas Mark 5, 10 minutes before baking. Lightly oil and line the base of an 18 cm/7 inch deep round cake tin with greaseproof or baking paper.

Mash 2 of the bananas in a small bowl, sprinkle with the lemon juice and a heaped tablespoon of the sugar. Mix together lightly and reserve.

Gently heat the remaining sugar and butter or margarine in a small saucepan until the butter has just melted. Pour into a small bowl, then allow to cool slightly. Sift the flour and cinnamon into a large bowl and make a well in the centre.

Beat the eggs into the cooled sugar mixture, pour into the well of flour and mix thoroughly.

Gently stir in the mashed banana mixture. Pour half of the mixture into the prepared tin. Thinly slice the remaining banana and arrange over the cake mixture. Sprinkle over the chopped walnuts, then cover with the remaining cake mixture.

Bake in the preheated oven for 50–55 minutes until well risen and golden. Allow to cool in the tin, turn out and sprinkle with the ground cinnamon and caster sugar. Serve hot or cold with fresh cream for pouring.

FRUIT CAKE

Cuts into 10 slices

225 g/8 oz butter or margarine
200 g/7 oz soft brown sugar
finely grated zest of 1 orange
1 tbsp black treacle
3 large eggs, beaten
275 g/10 oz plain flour
$1/_4$ tsp ground cinnamon
$1/_2$ tsp mixed spice
pinch freshly grated nutmeg
$1/_4$ tsp bicarbonate of soda
75 g/3 oz mixed peel
50 g/2 oz glacé cherries
125 g/4 oz raisins
125 g/4 oz sultanas
125 g/4 oz ready-to-eat dried
apricots, chopped

Preheat the oven to 150°C/300°F/Gas Mark 2, 10 minutes before baking. Lightly oil and line a 23 cm/9 inch deep round cake tin with a double thickness of greaseproof paper.

In a large bowl, cream together the butter or margarine, sugar and orange zest, until light and fluffy, then beat in the treacle. Beat in the eggs a little at a time, beating well between each addition.

Reserve 1 tablespoon of the flour. Sift the remaining flour, the spices and bicarbonate of soda into the mixture.

Mix all the fruits and the reserved flour together, then stir into the cake mixture. Turn into the prepared tin and smooth the top, making a small hollow in the centre of the cake mixture. Bake in the preheated oven for 1 hour, then reduce the heat to 140°C/275°F/Gas Mark 1.

Bake for a further $1^1/_2$ hours, or until cooked and a skewer inserted into the centre comes out clean. Leave to cool in the tin, then turn the cake out and serve.

DUNDEE CAKE

❧

Serves 8–10

400 g/14 oz mixed dried fruit
50 g/2 oz ground almonds
finely grated zest and juice of
1 lemon
150 g/5 oz butter, at room
temperature
150 g/5 oz natural golden
caster sugar
3 medium eggs, beaten
125 g/4 oz plain flour
40 g/1½ oz whole blanched
almonds

Preheat the oven to 180°C/350°F/Gas Mark 4. Grease and line the base of an 18 cm/7 inch deep round cake tin with nonstick baking parchment.

Place the dried fruits in a bowl and stir in the ground almonds to coat the dried fruit.

Grate the zest finely from the lemon into the bowl, then squeeze out 1 tablespoon of juice and add to the same bowl. In another bowl, beat the butter and sugar together until light and fluffy. Whisk in the eggs a little at a time, adding 1 teaspoon of flour with each addition.

Sift in the remaining flour, then add the fruit and almond mixture. Fold together with a large metal spoon until smooth. Spoon the mixture into the tin and make a dip in the centre with the back of a spoon. Arrange the almonds over the top in circles.

Bake for 1 hour, then reduce the heat to 150°C/300°F/Gas Mark 2 and bake for a further, hour or until a skewer inserted into the centre comes out clean. Cool in the tin for 5 minutes, then turn out to cool on a wire rack.

LEMON DRIZZLE CAKE

❦

Cuts into 16 slices

125 g/4 oz butter or margarine
175 g/6 oz caster sugar
2 large eggs
175 g/6 oz self-raising flour
2 lemons, preferably unwaxed
50 g/2 oz granulated sugar

Preheat the oven to 180°C/350°F/Gas Mark 4, 10 minutes before baking. Lightly oil and line the base of an 18 cm/7 inch square cake tin with baking paper.

In a large bowl, cream the butter or margarine and sugar together until soft and fluffy. Beat the eggs, then gradually add a little of the egg to the creamed mixture, adding 1 tablespoon of flour after each addition.

Finely grate the zest from 1 of the lemons and stir into the creamed mixture, beating well until smooth. Squeeze the juice from the lemon, strain, then stir into the mixture. Spoon into the prepared tin, level the surface and bake in the preheated oven for 25–30 minutes. Using a zester, remove the peel from the last lemon and mix with 25 g/1 oz of the granulated sugar and reserve.

Squeeze the juice into a small saucepan. Add the rest of the granulated sugar to the lemon juice in the saucepan and heat gently, stirring occasionally. When the sugar has dissolved, simmer gently for 3–4 minutes until syrupy.

With a cocktail stick or fine skewer, prick the cake all over. Sprinkle the lemon zest and sugar over the top of the cake, drizzle over the syrup and leave to cool in the tin. Cut the cake into squares and serve.

TOFFEE APPLE CAKE

Cuts into 8 slices

2 small eating apples, peeled
4 tbsp soft dark brown sugar
175 g/6 oz butter or margarine
175 g/6 oz caster sugar
3 medium eggs
175 g/6 oz self-raising flour
150 ml/^{1}/$_4$ pint double cream
2 tbsp icing sugar
^{1}/$_2$ tsp vanilla extract
^{1}/$_2$ tsp ground cinnamon

Preheat the oven to 180°C/350°F/Gas Mark 4, 10 minutes before baking time. Lightly oil and line the bases of 2 x 20.5 cm/8 inch sandwich tins with greaseproof or baking paper.

Thinly slice the apples and toss in the brown sugar until well coated. Arrange them over the bases of the prepared tins and reserve.

Cream together the butter or margarine and caster sugar until light and fluffy.

Beat the eggs together in a small bowl and gradually beat them into the creamed mixture, beating well between each addition. Sift the flour into the mixture and, using a metal spoon or rubber spatula, fold in.

Divide the mixture between the two cake tins and level the surface. Bake in the preheated oven for 25–30 minutes until golden and well risen. Leave in the tins to cool.

Lightly whip the cream with 1 tablespoon of the icing sugar and the vanilla extract. Sandwich the cakes together with the cream. Mix the remaining icing sugar and the ground cinnamon together, sift over the top of the cake and serve.

HONEY CAKE

❧

Cuts into 6 slices

50 g/2 oz butter
25 g/1 oz caster sugar
125 g/4 oz clear honey
175 g/6 oz plain flour
1/2 tsp bicarbonate of soda
1/2 tsp mixed spice
1 medium egg
2 tbsp milk
25 g/1 oz flaked almonds
1 tbsp clear honey, to drizzle

Preheat the oven to 180°C/350°F/Gas Mark 4, 10 minutes before baking. Lightly oil and line the base of an 18 cm/7 inch deep round cake tin with lightly oiled greaseproof or baking parchment.

In a saucepan, gently heat the butter, sugar and honey until the butter has just melted.

Sift the flour, bicarbonate of soda and mixed spice together into a bowl.

Beat the egg and the milk until mixed thoroughly.

Make a well in the centre of the sifted flour and pour in the melted butter and honey. Using a wooden spoon, beat well, gradually drawing in the flour from the sides of the bowl. When all the flour has been beaten in, add the egg mixture and mix thoroughly. Pour into the prepared tin and sprinkle with the flaked almonds.

Bake in the preheated oven for 30–35 minutes until well risen and golden brown and a skewer inserted into the centre of the cake comes out clean.

Remove from the oven and cool for a few minutes in the tin before turning out and leaving to cool on a wire rack. Drizzle with the remaining tablespoon of honey and serve.

GINGERBREAD

❧

Cuts into 8 slices

175 g/6 oz butter or margarine
225 g/8 oz black treacle
50 g/2 oz dark muscovado sugar
350 g/12 oz plain flour
2 tsp ground ginger
150 ml/¼ pint milk, warmed
2 medium eggs
1 tsp bicarbonate of soda
1 piece stem ginger in syrup
1 tbsp stem ginger syrup

Preheat the oven to 150°C/300°F/Gas Mark 2, 10 minutes before baking. Lightly oil and line the base of a 20.5 cm/8 inch deep round cake tin with greaseproof or baking paper.

In a saucepan, gently heat the butter or margarine, black treacle and sugar, stirring occasionally, until the butter melts. Leave to cool slightly.

Sift the flour and ground ginger into a large bowl. Make a well in the centre, then pour in the treacle mixture. Reserve 1 tablespoon of the milk, then pour the rest into the treacle mixture. Stir together lightly until mixed.

Beat the eggs together, then stir into the mixture.

Dissolve the bicarbonate of soda in the remaining 1 tablespoon of warmed milk and add to the mixture. Beat the mixture until well mixed and free of lumps. Pour into the prepared tin and bake in the preheated oven for 1 hour, or until well risen and a skewer inserted into the centre comes out clean.

Cool in the tin, then remove. Slice the stem ginger into thin slivers and sprinkle over the cake. Drizzle with the syrup and serve.

DROP SCONES

❧

Makes 18 scones

white vegetable fat, for greasing
175 g/6 oz self-raising flour
1 tsp baking powder
40 g/1½ oz caster sugar
1 medium egg
200 ml/7 fl oz milk
butter and syrup, to serve

Grease a heavy-based nonstick frying pan or a flat griddle pan with white vegetable fat and heat gently.

Sift the flour and baking powder into a bowl, stir in the sugar and make a well in the centre. Add the egg and half the milk and beat to a smooth thick batter. Beat in enough of the remaining milk to give the consistency of thick cream.

Drop the mixture onto the hot pan 1 heaped tablespoon at a time, spacing them well apart. When small bubbles rise to the surface of each scone, flip them over with a palette knife and cook for about 1 minute until golden brown.

Place on a serving dish and keep warm, covered with a clean cloth, while you cook the remaining mixture. Serve warm with butter and syrup and eat on the day of making.

EASY DANISH PASTRIES

❧

Makes 16

500 g/1 lb 2 oz strong white flour
1/2 tsp salt
350 g/12 oz butter
7 g sachet fast-action yeast
50 g/2 oz caster sugar
150 ml/1/4 pint lukewarm milk
2 medium eggs, beaten

For the filling and topping:

225 g/8 oz almond paste, grated
(see page 36)
8 canned apricot halves, drained
1 egg, beaten
125 g/4 oz fondant icing sugar
50 g/2 oz glacé cherries
50 g/2 oz flaked almonds

Sift the flour and salt into a bowl, add 50 g/2 oz of the butter and rub in until the mixture resembles fine crumbs, then stir in the yeast and sugar. Stir in the milk and beaten eggs and mix to a soft dough. Knead by hand for 10 minutes until smooth. Cover with oiled clingfilm and leave for 1 hour in a warm place or until doubled in size. Place the dough on a floured surface and knead to knock out the air for about 4 minutes until smooth. Roll out into a rectangle 20 x 35 cm/8 x 14 inches. Dot two thirds of the dough with half the remaining butter, leaving one third plain. Fold the plain third up over the buttered section, then fold the top third over this to form a square parcel. Press the edges to seal, then turn the dough, with the fold to the left. Roll out again to a rectangle and dot with the remaining butter as before. Chill for 15 minutes, then roll out and fold again. Roll, fold and chill once more.

Preheat the oven to 220°C/425°F/Gas Mark 7. Roll out the dough into a 55 cm/22 inch square and cut into 16 squares. Put 25 g/1 oz of the grated almond paste in the centre of each. Take eight of the squares and cut the corners almost to the middle and fold over the alternate points. Top each of the remaining squares with an apricot half and fold the opposite corners over to cover the apricots. Arrange all the pastries on buttered baking sheets and leave to rise for 20 minutes until puffy. Brush with beaten egg and bake for 15 minutes until golden. When cold, mix the fondant icing sugar with water to make a smooth icing. Drizzle over the pastries and place a halved cherry on the windmill shapes. Scatter the apricot-filled pastries with flaked almonds and leave to set for 30 minutes.

JAMMY BUNS

❦

Makes 12

175 g/6 oz plain flour
175 g/6 oz wholemeal flour
2 tsp baking powder
150 g/5 oz butter or margarine
125 g/4 oz golden caster sugar
50 g/2 oz dried cranberries
1 large egg, beaten
1 tbsp milk
4–5 tbsp seedless raspberry jam

Preheat the oven to 190°C/375°F/Gas Mark 5, 10 minutes before baking. Lightly oil a large baking sheet.

Sift the flours and baking powder together into a large bowl, then tip in the grains remaining in the sieve.

Cut the butter or margarine into small pieces. (It is easier to do this when the butter is in the flour, as it helps stop the butter from sticking to the knife.) Rub the butter into the flours until it resembles coarse breadcrumbs. Stir in the sugar and cranberries.

Using a round-bladed knife, stir in the beaten egg and milk. Mix to form a firm dough. Divide the mixture into 12 and roll into balls.

Place the dough balls on the baking tray, leaving enough space for expansion. Press the thumb into the centre of each ball, making a small hollow. Spoon a little of the jam in each hollow. Pinch lightly to seal the tops. Bake in the preheated oven for 20–25 minutes until golden brown. Cool on a wire rack and serve.

EASY CHOCOLATE CAKE

Serves 8–10

75 g/3 oz dark chocolate, broken
into squares
200 ml/7 fl oz milk
250 g/9 oz dark muscovado sugar
75 g/3 oz butter, softened
2 medium eggs, beaten
150 g/5 oz plain flour
$\frac{1}{2}$ tsp vanilla extract
1 tsp bicarbonate of soda
25 g/1 oz cocoa powder

For the topping and filling:

125 g/4 oz unsalted butter
225 g/8 oz icing sugar, sifted
175 g/6 oz fresh strawberries, halved
tiny mint sprigs, to decorate

Preheat the oven to 180°C/350°F/Gas Mark 4. Grease two 20.5 cm/8 inch round sandwich tins and line the bases with nonstick baking parchment. Place the chocolate, milk and 75 g/3 oz of the sugar in a heavy-based saucepan. Heat gently until the mixture has melted, then set aside to cool.

Place the butter and remaining sugar in a large bowl and whisk with an electric mixer until light and fluffy. Gradually whisk in the eggs, adding 1 teaspoon flour with each addition. Stir in the cooled melted chocolate mixture along with the vanilla extract. Sift in the flour, bicarbonate of soda and cocoa powder, then fold into the mixture until smooth.

Spoon the batter into the tins and smooth level. Bake for about 30 minutes until a skewer inserted in the centre comes out clean. Turn out to cool on a wire rack.

To decorate, beat the butter with the icing sugar and 1 tablespoon warm water until light and fluffy, then place half in a piping bag fitted with a star nozzle. Spread half the buttercream over one sponge layer and scatter half the strawberries over it. Top with the other cake and spread the remaining buttercream over the top. Pipe a border of stars around the edge. Decorate with the remaining strawberries and mint sprigs.

COFFEE & PECAN CAKE

Cuts into 8 slices

175 g/6 oz self-raising flour
125 g/4 oz butter or margarine
175 g/6 oz golden caster sugar
1 tbsp instant coffee powder
or granules
2 large eggs
50 g/2 oz pecans, roughly chopped

For the icing:

75 g/3 oz unsalted butter, softened
175 g/6 oz icing sugar, sifted
1 tsp instant coffee powder
or granules
1 tsp cocoa powder
whole pecans, to decorate

Preheat the oven to 190°C/375°F/Gas Mark 5, 10 minutes before baking. Lightly oil and line the bases of two 18 cm/7 inch sandwich tins with greaseproof or baking paper. Sift the flour and reserve.

Beat the butter or margarine and sugar together until light and creamy. Dissolve the coffee in 2 tablespoons hot water and allow to cool.

Lightly mix the eggs with the coffee liquid. Gradually beat into the creamed butter and sugar, adding a little of the sifted flour with each addition.

Fold in the pecans, then divide the mixture between the prepared tins and bake in the preheated oven for 20–25 minutes until well risen and firm to the touch. Leave to cool in the tins for 5 minutes before turning out and cooling on a wire rack.

To make the icing, beat together the butter and icing sugar. Then blend together the coffee and cocoa powder with enough boiling water to make a stiff paste. Beat into the butter and icing sugar.

Sandwich the 2 cakes together using half of the icing. Spread the remaining icing over the top of the cake and decorate with the whole pecans to serve.

CHOCOLATE NUT BROWNIES

Makes 16

125 g/4 oz butter
150 g/5 oz soft light brown sugar,
firmly packed
50 g/2 oz plain dark chocolate,
roughly chopped or broken
2 tbsp smooth peanut butter
2 medium eggs
50 g/2 oz unsalted roasted peanuts,
finely chopped
100 g/3^1/$_2$ oz self-raising flour

For the topping:

125 g/4 oz plain dark chocolate,
roughly chopped or broken
50 ml/2 fl oz sour cream

Preheat the oven to 180°C/350°F/Gas Mark 4, 10 minutes before baking. Lightly oil and line a 20.5 cm/8 inch square cake tin with greaseproof or baking paper.

Combine the butter, sugar and chocolate in a small saucepan and heat gently until the sugar and chocolate have melted, stirring constantly. Reserve and cool slightly.

Mix together the peanut butter, eggs and peanuts in a large bowl. Stir in the cooled chocolate mixture. Sift in the flour and fold together with a metal spoon or rubber spatula until combined. Pour into the prepared tin and bake in the preheated oven for about 30 minutes until just firm. Cool for 5 minutes in the tin before turning out onto a wire rack to cool.

To make the topping, melt the chocolate in a heatproof bowl over a saucepan of simmering water, making sure that the base of the bowl does not touch the water. Cool slightly, then stir in the sour cream until smooth and glossy. Spread over the brownies, refrigerate until set, then cut into squares. Serve the brownies cold.

BUTTERSCOTCH LOAF

Serves 8

1 banana, peeled, weighing about
100 g/3¹/₂ oz
125 g/4 oz soft margarine
125 g/4 oz golden caster sugar
2 medium eggs
1 tsp almond extract
¹/₂ tsp vanilla extract
125 g/4 oz self-raising flour
75 g/3 oz dark chocolate chips
75 g/3 oz walnuts, chopped

To decorate:

50 g/2 oz natural icing sugar
25 g/1 oz golden lump sugar

Preheat the oven to 170°C/325°F/Gas Mark 3. Grease and line the base of a 1 kg/2 lb 3 oz loaf tin with a long thin strip of nonstick baking parchment.

Place the banana in a bowl and mash. Add the margarine, sugar and eggs along with the extracts and sift in the flour. Beat until smooth, then stir in the chocolate chips and add half the chopped walnuts. Stir until smooth, then spoon into the tin and spread level.

Bake for about 45 minutes until a skewer inserted into the centre comes out clean. Leave in the tin for 5 minutes, then turn out to cool on a wire rack, peel away the paper and leave to cool.

To decorate, make the icing sugar into a runny consistency with 2 teaspoons water. Drizzle over the cake and sprinkle over the remaining walnuts and the sugar lumps. Leave to set for 30 minutes, then serve sliced.

MARMALADE LOAF CAKE

❦

Serves 8–10

175 g/6 oz natural golden caster sugar
175 g/6 oz butter, softened
3 medium eggs, beaten
175 g/6 oz self-raising flour
finely grated zest and juice of 1 orange
100 g/3½ oz orange marmalade

For the topping:

zest and juice of 1 orange
125 g/4 oz icing sugar

Preheat the oven to 180°C/350°F/Gas Mark 4. Grease and line a 1 kg/2 lb 3 oz loaf tin with a long thin strip of nonstick baking parchment.

Place the sugar and butter in a bowl and whisk until light and fluffy. Add the beaten egg a little at a time, adding 1 teaspoon flour with each addition.

Add the remaining flour to the bowl with the orange zest, 2 tablespoons orange juice and the marmalade. Using a large metal spoon, fold the mixture together using a figure-of-eight movement until all the flour is incorporated. Spoon the batter into the tin and smooth level.

Bake for about 40 minutes until firm in the centre and a skewer inserted into the centre comes out clean. Cool in the tin for 5 minutes, then turn out to cool on a wire rack.

To make the topping, peel thin strips of zest away from the orange and set aside. Squeeze the juice from the orange. Sift the icing sugar into a bowl and mix with 1 tablespoon orange juice until a thin smooth consistency forms. Drizzle over the top of the cake, letting it run down the sides. Scatter over the orange zest and leave to set for 1 hour.

CUPCAKES

& MUFFINS

The fun alternative to classic cakes are beautiful and enticing individual cupcakes, or chunky, moreish muffins. Here, learn how to create delicate sponge Raspberry Butterfly Cupcakes or decadent Chocolate and Toffee Cupcakes; or have some fun with colours and shapes by making Fondant Fancies or Polka Dot Cupcakes. For a tasty muffin that you just want to get your teeth into, try the indulgent Cappuccino Muffins.

MADELEINE CUPCAKES

❧

Makes 10–12

125 g/4 oz self-raising flour
125 g/4 oz butter, softened
125 g/4 oz golden caster sugar
2 medium eggs, beaten
1 tsp vanilla extract

To decorate:

4 tbsp seedless raspberry jam
65 g/2½ oz desiccated coconut
glacé cherries, halved

Preheat the oven to 180°C/350°F/Gas Mark 4. Line a 12-hole muffin tray with 10–12 paper cases, depending on the depth of the holes.

Sift the flour into a bowl and add the butter, sugar, eggs and extract. Beat for about 2 minutes until smooth, then spoon into the paper cases.

Bake in the centre of the oven for about 14–16 minutes until well risen and springy in the centre. Transfer to a wire rack to cool.

To decorate the cupcakes, warm the raspberry jam in a small pan or in the microwave oven in a heatproof dish on low for a few seconds. Brush the warmed jam over the top of each cupcake. Lightly coat the top of each cupcake with coconut, then finish with a halved cherry.

DOUBLE CHERRY CUPCAKES

༺༒༻

Makes 12 large cupcakes or 18 fairy cakes

50 g/2 oz glacé cherries, washed, dried and chopped
125 g/4 oz self-raising flour
25 g/1 oz dried morello cherries
125 g/4 oz soft margarine
125 g/4 oz caster sugar
2 medium eggs
$\frac{1}{2}$ tsp almond extract

To decorate:

125 g/4 oz fondant icing sugar
pale pink liquid food colouring
40 g/1$\frac{1}{2}$ oz glacé cherries

Preheat the oven to 190°C/375°F/Gas Mark 5. Line a 12-hole muffin tray with deep paper cases, or two trays with 18 fairy-cake cases.

Dust the chopped glacé cherries lightly in a tablespoon of the flour, then mix with the morello cherries and set aside. Sift the rest of the flour into a bowl, then add the margarine, sugar, eggs and almond extract. Beat for about 2 minutes until smooth, then fold in the cherries.

Spoon the batter into the paper cases and bake for 15–20 minutes until well risen and springy in the centre. Turn out to cool on a wire rack.

To decorate the cupcakes, trim the tops level. Mix the icing sugar with 2–3 teaspoons warm water and a few drops of pink food colouring to make a thick consistency. Spoon the icing over each cupcake filling right up to the edge. Chop the cherries finely and sprinkle over the icing.

Leave to set for 30 minutes.

RASPBERRY BUTTERFLY CUPCAKES

❧

Makes 12–14

125 g/4 oz caster sugar
125 g/4 oz soft tub margarine
2 medium eggs
125 g/4 oz self-raising flour
1/2 tsp baking powder
1/2 tsp vanilla extract

To decorate:

4 tbsp seedless raspberry jam
12–14 fresh raspberries
icing sugar, to dust

Preheat the oven to 190°C/375°F/Gas Mark 5. Line one or two bun trays with 12–14 paper cases, depending on the depth of the holes.

Place all the cupcake ingredients in a large bowl and beat with an electric mixer for about 2 minutes until smooth. Fill the paper cases halfway up with the mixture.

Bake for about 15 minutes until firm, risen and golden. Remove to a wire rack to cool.

When cold, cut a small circle out of the top of each cupcake and then cut the circle in half to form wings.

Fill each cupcake with a teaspoon of raspberry jam. Replace the wings at an angle and top each with a fresh raspberry. Dust lightly with icing sugar and serve immediately.

FONDANT FANCIES

Makes 16–18

150 g/5 oz self-raising flour
150 g/5 oz caster sugar
50 g/2 oz ground almonds
150 g/5 oz butter, softened
3 medium eggs, beaten
4 tbsp milk

To decorate:

450 g/1 lb fondant icing sugar
paste food colourings
selection fancy cake decorations

Preheat the oven to 180°C/350°F/Gas Mark 4. Line two 12-hole bun trays with 16–18 paper cases, depending on the depth of the holes.

Sift the flour into a bowl and stir in the caster sugar and almonds. Add the butter, eggs and milk and beat until smooth.

Spoon into the paper cases and bake for 15–20 minutes until golden and firm to the touch. Turn out to cool on a wire rack. When cool, trim the tops flat if they have peaked slightly.

To decorate the cupcakes, make the fondant icing to a thick coating consistency, following the packet instructions. Divide into batches and colour each separately with a little paste food colouring. Keep each bowl covered with a damp cloth until needed. Spoon some icing over each cupcake, being sure to flood it right to the edge. Top each with a fancy decoration and leave to set for 30 minutes.

SHAGGY COCONUT CUPCAKES

Makes 12

¹/₂ tsp baking powder
200 g/7 oz self-raising flour
175 g/6 oz caster sugar
2 tbsp desiccated coconut
175 g/6 oz soft margarine
3 medium eggs, beaten
2 tbsp milk

To decorate:

1 batch buttercream (*see page 32*)
1 tbsp coconut liqueur (optional)
175 g/6 oz large shredded
coconut strands

Preheat the oven to 180°C/350°F/Gas Mark 4. Line a 12-hole deep muffin tray with paper cases.

Sift the baking powder and flour into a large bowl. Add all the remaining ingredients and beat for about 2 minutes until smooth and creamy. Divide evenly between the paper cases.

Bake for 18–20 minutes until risen, golden and firm to the touch. Leave in the muffin trays for 2 minutes, then turn out to cool on a wire rack.

To decorate the cupcakes, if you are using the coconut liqueur, beat this into the buttercream and then swirl over each cupcake. To decorate, press large strands of shredded coconut into the buttercream.

COFFEE & WALNUT FUDGE CUPCAKES

⚜

Makes 16–18

125 g/4 oz self-raising flour
125 g/4 oz butter, softened
125 g/4 oz golden caster sugar
2 medium eggs
1 tbsp golden syrup
50 g/2 oz walnuts, finely chopped

To decorate:

225 g/8 oz golden icing sugar
125 g/4 oz unsalted butter,
at room temperature
2 tsp coffee extract
16–18 small walnut pieces

Preheat the oven to 200°C/400°F/Gas Mark 6. Line two 12-hole bun trays with 16–18 small foil cases, depending on the depth of the tray holes.

Sift the flour into a bowl and add the butter, sugar, eggs and syrup. Beat for about 2 minutes, then fold in the walnuts.

Spoon the mixture into the paper cases and bake for about 12–14 minutes until well risen and springy in the centre. Remove to a wire rack to cool.

Make the frosting by sifting the icing sugar into a bowl. Add the butter, coffee extract and 1 tablespoon hot water. Beat until light and fluffy, then place in a piping bag fitted with a star nozzle. Pipe a swirl on each cupcake and top with a walnut piece.

CHOCOLATE &
TOFFEE CUPCAKES

Makes 12–14

125 g/4 oz soft fudge
125 g/4 oz soft margarine
125 g/4 oz golden caster sugar
150 g/5 oz self-raising flour
2 tbsp cocoa powder
2 medium eggs
1 tbsp golden syrup
1 batch cream cheese frosting
(*see* page 32),
to decorate

Preheat the oven to 180°C/350°F/Gas Mark 4. Line one or two bun trays with 12–14 paper cases, depending on the depth of the holes. Cut one quarter of the fudge into slices for decoration. Chop the rest into small cubes. Set all the fudge aside.

Place the margarine and the sugar in a large bowl and then sift in the flour and cocoa powder. In another bowl, beat the eggs with the syrup, then add to the flour mixture.

Whisk together with an electric beater for 2 minutes, or by hand with a wooden spoon until smooth. Gently fold in the fudge cubes.

Spoon the mixture into the cases, filling them three-quarters full. Bake for about 15 minutes until a skewer inserted into the centre comes out clean. Turn out to cool on a wire rack.

Swirl the cream cheese frosting over each cupcake, then finish by topping with a fudge slice.

CAPPUCCINO MUFFINS

❦

Makes 12–14

125 g/4 oz soft margarine
125 g/4 oz golden caster sugar
150 g/5 oz self-raising flour
2 tbsp cocoa powder
2 medium eggs
1 tbsp golden syrup
50 g/2 oz finely grated chocolate

To decorate:

150 ml/¼ pint double cream
chocolate sprinkles

Preheat the oven to 180°C/350°F/Gas Mark 4. Line one or two bun trays with 12–14 paper cases or silicone moulds, depending on the depth of the holes.

Place the margarine and the sugar in a large bowl, then sift in the flour and cocoa powder.

In another bowl, beat the eggs with the syrup, then add to the flour mixture. Whisk together with an electric beater for 2 minutes, or by hand with a wooden spoon until smooth and then fold in the grated chocolate.

Divide the mixture between the cases, filling them three-quarters full. Bake for about 20 minutes until springy to the touch in the centre. Turn out to cool on a wire rack.

For the decoration, whisk the cream until it forms soft peaks, then swirl over the tops of the muffins with a small palette knife. Scatter the tops with chocolate sprinkles to serve.

ORANGE DRIZZLE CUPCAKES

Makes 10

75 g/3 oz dark chocolate, chopped
125 g/4 oz butter
125 g/4 oz caster sugar
2 medium eggs, beaten
200 g/7 oz self-raising flour
zest of $^1/_2$ orange, finely grated
5 tbsp thick natural yogurt

To decorate:

1 batch orange-flavoured
buttercream (*see* page 32)
2 tbsp marmalade

Preheat the oven to 190°C/375°F/Gas Mark 5. Grease 10 deep muffin moulds or line a 12-hole muffin tray with 10 deep paper cases.

Melt the chocolate in a heatproof bowl over a pan of warm water or in the microwave oven on low for 30 seconds and leave to cool.

Put the butter and sugar in a large bowl and whisk until light and fluffy. Gradually beat in the eggs, adding a teaspoon of flour with each addition. Beat in the cooled melted chocolate, then sift in the flour. Add the orange zest and yogurt to the bowl and whisk until smooth.

Spoon the mixture into the paper cases and bake for about 25 minutes until well risen and springy to the touch. Leave for 2 minutes in the moulds or tray, then turn out onto a wire rack.

To decorate, fill a piping bag fitted with a star nozzle with the buttercream and pipe swirls on top of each cupcake. Warm the marmalade and place small drizzles around the sides of the cupcakes with a teaspoon.

COLOURFUL LETTERS

Makes 12–14

125 g/4 oz self-raising flour
125 g/4 oz caster sugar
125 g/4 oz soft margarine
2 medium eggs, beaten
1 tsp vanilla extract

To decorate:

225 g/8 oz ready-to-roll sugarpaste
paste food colourings
350 g/12 oz icing sugar, sifted, plus
extra for dusting
small coloured sweets

Preheat the oven to 180°C/350°F/Gas Mark 4. Line two 12-hole bun trays with 12–14 paper fairy-cake cases or silicone moulds, depending on the depth of the holes.

Sift the flour into a bowl and stir together with the caster sugar. Add the margarine, eggs and vanilla extract and beat together for about 2 minutes until smooth.

Spoon into the cases and bake for 15–20 minutes until golden and firm to the touch. Turn out on a wire rack. When cool, trim the tops flat if they have peaked slightly.

To decorate, colour batches of sugarpaste in bright colours. Dust a clean surface lightly with icing sugar. Roll each colour out thinly and cut out letters using a set of cutters.

Blend the icing sugar with 1 tablespoon water to make a glacé icing of coating consistency. Spread over the top of each cupcake and place a bright letter in the centre of each one. Decorate round the edges with coloured sweets and leave the cupcakes to dry for 30 minutes.

JELLYBEAN CUPCAKES

Makes 12–14

125 g/4 oz self-raising flour
125 g/4 oz caster sugar
125 g/4 oz soft margarine
2 medium eggs, beaten
1 tsp vanilla extract

To decorate:

1 batch buttercream (*see* page 32)
colourful jellybeans or candied
jelly shapes

Preheat the oven to 180°C/350°F/Gas Mark 4. Line two 12-hole bun trays with 12–14 paper fairy-cake cases or silicone moulds, depending on the depth of the holes.

Sift the flour into a bowl and stir together with the caster sugar. Add the margarine, eggs and vanilla extract and beat together for about 2 minutes until smooth.

Spoon into the cases and bake for 15–20 minutes until golden and firm to the touch. Turn out to cool on a wire rack.

When completely cold, swirl buttercream icing all over the tops of the cupcakes and decorate by pressing on coloured jellybeans.

POLKA DOT CUPCAKES

❦

Makes 12

150 g/5 oz butter, softened
150 g/5 oz caster sugar
175 g/6 oz self-raising flour
3 medium eggs
1 tsp vanilla extract
2 tbsp milk

To decorate:

1 batch cream cheese frosting
(*see* page 32)
125 g/4 oz ready-to-roll sugarpaste
paste food colourings

Preheat the oven to 180°C/350°F/Gas Mark 4. Line a 12-hole muffin tray with paper or silicone cases.

Cream together the butter and sugar in a bowl, then sift in the flour. In another bowl, beat the eggs with the vanilla extract and milk, then add to the flour mixture and beat until smooth. Spoon into the cases, filling them three-quarters full.

Bake for about 18 minutes until firm to the touch in the centre. Turn out to cool on a wire rack.

To decorate the cupcakes, swirl the top of each cupcake with a little cream cheese icing, using a small palette knife. Divide the sugarpaste into batches and colour each one separately with paste food colouring. Dust a clean flat surface with icing sugar. Roll out the coloured icing and stamp out small coloured circles with the flat end of an icing nozzle. Press the dots onto the frosting.

PISTACHIO MUFFINS

❀

Makes 10

125 g/4 oz self-raising flour
125 g/4 oz butter, softened
125 g/4 oz golden caster sugar
2 medium eggs, beaten
1 tbsp maple syrup or golden syrup
50 g/2 oz pistachio nuts,
roughly chopped

To decorate:

225 g/8 oz golden icing sugar
125 g/4 oz unsalted butter, softened
2 tsp lemon juice
25 g/1 oz pistachio nuts, chopped

Preheat the oven to 200°C/400°F/Gas Mark 6. Line a deep 12-hole muffin tray with 10 deep paper cases.

Sift the flour into a bowl and add the butter, sugar and eggs. Beat for about 2 minutes, then fold in the syrup and chopped nuts.

Spoon the mixture into the paper cases and bake for about 20 minutes until well risen and springy in the centre. Remove to a wire rack to cool.

To decorate the cakes, sift the icing sugar into a bowl, then add the butter, lemon juice and 1 tablespoon hot water. Beat until light and fluffy, then swirl onto each cupcake with a small palette knife. Place the chopped pistachio nuts in a small shallow bowl. Dip the top of each muffin into the nuts to make an attractive topping.

BISCUITS

& COOKIES

Why not make your own biscuits to have with your tea? Here, you have got a raft of essential recipes that every baker should know, from cookies, such as Peanut Butter Truffle Cookies and Chocolate Chip Cookies, to classic melt-in-the-mouth shortbread-type biscuits such as Viennese Fingers; from fun jammy Traffic Lights and different kinds of macaroon, to flapjacks and gingerbread – which will you choose first?

TRAFFIC LIGHTS

Makes 14

125 g/4 oz butter, softened
75 g/3 oz caster sugar
25 g/1 oz golden syrup
1 medium egg, beaten
few drops vanilla extract
275 g/10 oz plain flour, plus extra
for dusting
1 tsp baking powder

To decorate:

4 tbsp strawberry jam
4 tbsp apricot jam
4 tbsp lime marmalade
icing sugar, for dredging

Preheat the oven to 180°C/350°F/Gas Mark 4. Grease two baking trays. Beat the butter, sugar and syrup together until light and fluffy.

Gradually beat in the egg and vanilla extract. Sift the flour and baking powder into the bowl and stir into the mixture. Gather the mixture up with your hands and work it into a dough. Turn out onto a floured surface and knead gently until smooth. Wrap in clingfilm for 30 minutes and chill.

Roll the pastry out to a thickness of 3 mm/$\frac{1}{8}$ inch and cut into 28 oblongs measuring 3 x 8.5 cm/1$\frac{1}{4}$ x 3$\frac{1}{2}$ inches. Using the broad end of a piping nozzle or a cutter measuring 2 cm/$\frac{3}{4}$ inch wide, cut out three holes in each of 14 of the oblongs, remove the cut-out discs and discard or re-roll to use as pastry trimmings. Place all the oblongs on the baking sheets and bake for 8–10 minutes until golden. Transfer to a wire rack to cool.

Place 3 small teaspoonfuls of different coloured jams along the centre of each rectangular biscuit, starting with strawberry for red at the top, apricot for amber in the middle and lime marmalade for green at the base. Dust the biscuits with the round holes with icing sugar. Position these over the jam on the rectangular biscuits and press down so that the jam shows through.

CHERRY GARLANDS

❦

Makes 30

125 g/4 oz plain flour
pinch salt
65 g/2¹/₂ oz butter, softened
50 g/2 oz caster sugar
1 egg yolk
¹/₂ tsp almond extract

To decorate:

12 glacé cherries
1 egg white, lightly beaten
caster sugar

Preheat the oven to 190°C/375°F/Gas Mark 5 and grease two baking sheets. Sift the flour and salt into a bowl or a food processor, add the butter and rub in with fingertips or process until the mixture resembles fine crumbs. Stir in the sugar.

In another bowl, beat the egg yolk with the almond extract and add to the flour mixture. Stir to make a soft dough, then knead lightly. Roll the dough into pea-size balls and arrange 8 balls in a ring on a baking sheet, pressing them together lightly.

Continue making rings until all the dough is used up. Cut each glacé cherry into 8 tiny wedges and place 3 on each biscuit between the balls.

Bake for 14 minutes until golden, remove the biscuits from the oven and brush with beaten egg white. Sprinkle the tops lightly with caster sugar and return to the oven for 2 minutes until a sparkly glaze has formed. Leave to stand on the baking sheets for 2 minutes, then cool completely on a wire rack.

LEMON BUTTER BISCUITS

❀

Makes 14–18

175 g/6 oz butter, softened
75 g/3 oz caster sugar
175 g/6 oz plain flour
75 g/3 oz cornflour
zest of 1 lemon, finely grated
2 tbsp caster sugar, to decorate

Preheat the oven to 170°C/325°F/Gas Mark 3. Grease two baking sheets. Place the butter into a bowl and beat together with the sugar until light and fluffy.

Sift in the flour and cornflour, add the lemon zest and mix together with a flat-bladed knife to form a soft dough.

Place the dough on a lightly floured surface, knead lightly and roll out thinly. Use biscuit cutters to cut out fancy shapes, re-rolling the trimmings to make more biscuits. Carefully lift each biscuit onto a baking sheet with a palette knife, then prick lightly with a fork.

Bake for 12–15 minutes. Cool on the baking sheets for 5 minutes, then place on a wire rack. Once completely cool, dust with caster sugar.

MELTING MOMENTS

❧

Makes 16

125 g/4 oz butter, softened
75 g/3 oz caster sugar
$^1/_2$ tsp vanilla extract
150 g/5 oz self-raising flour
pinch salt
1 small egg or $^1/_2$ medium
egg, beaten
25 g/1 oz porridge oats
4 glacé cherries, quartered

Preheat the oven to 180°C/350°F/Gas Mark 4. Grease two baking sheets.

Beat the butter until light and fluffy, then whisk in the caster sugar and vanilla extract. Sift the flour and salt into the bowl. Add the egg and mix to a soft dough.

Break the dough into 16 pieces and roll each piece into a ball. Spread the oats out on a small flat bowl or plate. Roll each ball in the oats to coat them all over without flattening them.

Place a cherry quarter in the centre of each ball, then place on the baking sheets, spaced well apart. Bake for about 15 minutes until risen and golden. Remove from the baking sheets with a palette knife and cool on a wire rack.

CHOCOLATE CHIP COOKIES

❧

Makes 36 biscuits

175 g/6 oz plain flour
pinch salt
1 tsp baking powder
$^{1}/_{4}$ tsp bicarbonate of soda
75 g/3 oz butter or margarine
50 g/2 oz soft light brown sugar
3 tbsp golden syrup
125 g/4 oz chocolate chips

Preheat the oven to 190°C/375°F/Gas Mark 5, 10 minutes before baking. Lightly oil a large baking sheet.

In a large bowl, sift together the flour, salt, baking powder and bicarbonate of soda.

Cut the butter or margarine into small pieces and add to the flour mixture. Using two knives or the fingertips, rub in the butter or margarine until the mixture resembles coarse breadcrumbs.

Add the light brown sugar, golden syrup and chocolate chips. Mix together until a smooth dough forms.

Shape the mixture into small balls and arrange on the baking sheet, leaving enough space to allow them to expand. (These cookies do not increase in size by a great deal, but allow a little space for expansion.) Flatten the mixture slightly with the fingertips or the heel of the hand.

Bake in the preheated oven for 12–15 minutes until golden and cooked through. Allow to cool slightly, then transfer the biscuits onto a wire rack to cool.

CHOCOLATE & VANILLA RINGS

Makes 26

175 g/6 oz butter, softened
125 g/4 oz caster sugar
few drops vanilla extract
250 g/9 oz plain flour
15 g/1/2 oz cocoa powder
25 g/1 oz ground almonds

Preheat the oven to 180°C/350°F/Gas Mark 4 and grease two baking sheets.

Put the butter and sugar in a bowl and beat until light and fluffy. Add the vanilla extract, sift in the flour and mix to a soft dough. Divide the dough in two and add the cocoa powder to one half and the almonds to the other.

Knead each piece of dough separately into a smooth ball, wrap and chill for 30 minutes. Divide each piece into 26 pieces. Take one dark and one light ball and roll each separately into ropes about 12.5 cm/5 inches long using your fingers.

Twist the ropes together to form a circlet and pinch the ends together. Repeat with the remaining dough and place on a greased baking sheet. Bake for 12–14 minutes until risen and firm. Remove to cool on a wire rack.

PEANUT BUTTER TRUFFLE COOKIES

❦

Makes 18

125 g/4 oz dark chocolate
150 ml/^{1}/$_4$ pint double cream
125 g/4 oz butter or margarine,
softened
125 g/4 oz caster sugar
125 g/4 oz crunchy or smooth
peanut butter
4 tbsp golden syrup
1 tbsp milk
225 g/8 oz plain flour
^{1}/$_2$ tsp bicarbonate of soda

Preheat the oven to 180°C/350°F/Gas Mark 4, 10 minutes before baking. Make the chocolate filling by breaking the chocolate into small pieces and placing in a heatproof bowl.

Put the double cream into a saucepan and heat to boiling point. Immediately pour over the chocolate. Leave to stand for 1–2 minutes, then stir until smooth. Set aside to cool until firm enough to scoop. Do not refrigerate.

Lightly oil a baking sheet. Cream together the butter or margarine and the sugar until light and fluffy. Blend in the peanut butter, followed by the golden syrup and milk.

Sift together the flour and bicarbonate of soda. Add to the peanut butter mixture, mix well and knead until smooth.

Flatten 1–2 tablespoons of the cookie mixture on a chopping board. Put a spoonful of the chocolate mixture into the centre of the cookie dough, then fold the dough around the chocolate to enclose completely.

Put the balls onto the baking sheet and flatten slightly. Bake in the preheated oven for 10–12 minutes until golden. Remove from the oven and transfer to a wire rack to cool completely and serve.

GOLDEN HONEY FORK BISCUITS

❀

Makes 20–24 biscuits

125 g/4 oz butter or block
margarine, diced
125 g/4 oz soft light brown sugar
1 medium egg, beaten
$^1/_2$ tsp vanilla extract
2 tbsp clear honey
200 g/7 oz plain flour
$^1/_2$ tsp baking powder
$^1/_2$ tsp ground cinnamon

Preheat the oven to 180°C/350°F/Gas Mark 4. Grease two baking sheets.

Place the butter and sugar in a bowl and beat together until light and fluffy. Beat in the egg, a little at a time, and then beat in the vanilla extract and honey.

Sift the flour, baking powder and cinnamon into the bowl and fold into the mixture with a large metal spoon.

Put heaped teaspoons of the mixture onto the prepared baking sheets, leaving room for them to spread out during baking. Press the top of each round with the tines of a fork to make a light indentation.

Bake for 10–12 minutes until golden. Cool for 2 minutes on the baking sheets, then transfer to a wire rack to cool completely.

COCONUT MACAROONS

✿

Makes 18

rice paper
2 medium egg whites
125 g/4 oz icing sugar
125 g/4 oz desiccated coconut
125 g/4 oz ground almonds
zest of $^1/_2$ lemon or lime,
finely grated

Preheat the oven to 180°C/350°F/Gas Mark 4. Line two baking sheets with rice paper.

Whisk the egg whites in a clean, dry bowl until soft peaks form. Using a large metal spoon, fold in the icing sugar. Fold in the coconut, almonds and lemon or lime zest until a sticky dough forms.

Heap dessertspoonfuls of the mixture onto the rice paper on the baking sheets. Bake for 10 minutes, then reduce the oven temperature to 150°C/300°F/Gas Mark 2.

Bake for a further 5–8 minutes until firm and golden, then remove to a wire rack to cool, breaking off any excess rice paper.

WHIPPED SHORTBREAD

❦

Makes 36

225 g/8 oz butter, softened
75 g/3 oz icing sugar
175 g/6 oz plain flour
hundreds and thousands
sugar strands
chocolate drops
silver balls
50 g/2 oz icing sugar
2–3 tsp lemon juice

Preheat the oven to 180°C/350°F/Gas Mark 4, 10 minutes before baking. Lightly oil a baking sheet.

Cream the butter and icing sugar together until fluffy. Gradually add the flour and continue beating for a further 2–3 minutes until smooth and light.

Roll into balls and place on a baking sheet. Cover half of the dough mixture with hundreds and thousands, sugar strands, chocolate drops or silver balls. Keep the other half plain.

Bake in the preheated oven for 6–8 minutes until the bottoms are lightly browned. Remove from the oven and transfer to a wire rack to cool.

Sift the icing sugar into a small bowl. Add the lemon juice and blend until a smooth icing forms.

Using a small spoon, swirl the icing over the cooled plain cookies. Decorate with the extra hundreds and thousands, sugar strands, chocolate drops or silver balls and serve.

VIENNESE FINGERS

Makes 28

225 g/8 oz butter, softened
75 g/3 oz icing sugar
1 medium egg, beaten
1 tsp vanilla extract
275 g/10 oz plain flour
1/2 tsp baking powder

To decorate:

4 tbsp sieved apricot jam
225 g/8 oz plain chocolate

Preheat the oven to 180°C/350°F/Gas Mark 4. Grease two baking sheets. Put the butter and icing sugar in a bowl and beat together until soft and fluffy.

Whisk in the egg and vanilla extract with 1 tablespoon of the flour. Sift in the remaining flour and the baking powder and beat with a wooden spoon to make a soft dough.

Place the mixture in a piping bag fitted with a large star nozzle and pipe into 6.5 cm/2¹/₂ inch lengths on the baking sheets. Bake for 15–20 minutes until pale golden and firm, then transfer to a wire rack to cool.

When cold, thinly spread one flat side of a biscuit with apricot jam and sandwich together with another biscuit.

To decorate the biscuits, break the chocolate into squares and place in a heatproof bowl and stand this over a pan of simmering water. Stir until the chocolate has melted, then dip the ends of the biscuits into the chocolate to coat. Leave on a wire rack for 1 hour until set.

PECAN CARAMEL MILLIONAIRE'S SHORTBREAD

Makes 20

125 g/4 oz butter, softened
2 tbsp smooth peanut butter
75 g/3 oz caster sugar
75 g/3 oz cornflour
175 g/6 oz plain flour

For the topping:

200 g/7 oz caster sugar
125 g/4 oz butter
2 tbsp golden syrup
75 ml/3 fl oz liquid glucose
75 ml/3 fl oz water
400 g can sweetened
condensed milk
175 g/6 oz pecans,
roughly chopped
75 g/3 oz dark chocolate
1 tbsp butter

Preheat the oven to 180°C/350°F/Gas Mark 4, 10 minutes before baking. Lightly oil and line an 18 x 28 cm/7 x 11 inch tin with greaseproof or baking paper.

Cream together the butter, peanut butter and sugar until light. Sift in the cornflour and flour together and mix in to make a smooth dough. Press the mixture into the tin and prick all over with a fork. Bake in the preheated oven for 20 minutes until just golden, then remove.

Meanwhile, for the topping, combine the sugar, butter, golden syrup, glucose, water and milk in a heavy-based saucepan. Stir constantly over a low heat without boiling until the sugar has dissolved. Increase the heat, boil steadily, stirring constantly, for about 10 minutes until the mixture turns a golden caramel colour.

Remove the saucepan from the heat and add the pecans. Pour over the shortbread base immediately. Allow to cool, then refrigerate for at least 1 hour.

Break the chocolate into small pieces and put into a heatproof bowl with the butter. Place over a saucepan of barely simmering water, ensuring that the bowl does not come into contact with the water. Leave until melted, then stir together well. Remove the shortbread from the refrigerator and pour the chocolate evenly over the top, spreading thinly to cover. Leave to set, cut into squares and serve.

GINGERBREAD BISCUITS

Makes 20 large or
28 small biscuits

225 g/8 oz plain flour, plus extra
for dusting
$1/2$ tsp ground ginger
$1/2$ tsp mixed spice
$1/2$ tsp bicarbonate of soda
75 g/3 oz butter
2 tbsp golden syrup
1 tbsp black treacle
75 g/3 oz soft dark brown sugar
50 g/2 oz royal icing sugar,
to decorate

Preheat the oven to 180°C/350°F/Gas Mark 4 and grease two baking sheets. Sift the flour, spices and bicarbonate of soda into a bowl.

Place the butter, syrup, treacle and sugar in a heavy-based pan with 1 tablespoon water and heat gently until every grain of sugar has dissolved and the butter has melted. Cool for 5 minutes, then pour the melted mixture into the dry ingredients and mix to a soft dough.

Leave the dough, covered, for 30 minutes. Roll out the dough on a lightly floured surface to a 3 mm/$1/8$ inch thickness and cut out fancy shapes. Gather up the trimmings and re-roll the dough, cutting out more shapes. Place on the baking sheets using a palette knife and bake for about 10 minutes until golden and firm. Be careful not to overcook, as the biscuits will brown quickly.

Decorate the biscuits by mixing the royal icing sugar with enough water to make a piping consistency. Place the icing in a small paper piping bag with the end snipped away and pipe faces and decorations onto the biscuits.

GINGER SNAPS

❦

Makes 10

300 g/11 oz butter or margarine, softened
225 g/8 oz soft light brown sugar
75 g/3 oz black treacle
1 medium egg
400 g/14 oz plain flour
2 tsp bicarbonate of soda
$1/2$ tsp salt
1 tsp ground ginger
1 tsp ground cloves
1 tsp ground cinnamon
50 g/2 oz granulated sugar

Preheat the oven to 190°C/375°F/Gas Mark 5, 10 minutes before baking. Lightly oil a baking sheet.

Cream together the butter or margarine and the sugar until light and fluffy.

Warm the treacle in the microwave for 30–40 seconds, then gradually add to the butter mixture with the egg. Beat until well combined.

In a separate bowl, sift the flour, bicarbonate of soda, salt, ground ginger, ground cloves and ground cinnamon. Add to the butter mixture and mix together to form a firm dough.

Chill in the refrigerator for 1 hour. Shape the dough into small balls and roll in the granulated sugar. Place well apart on the oiled baking sheet.

Sprinkle the baking sheet with a little water and transfer to the preheated oven.

Bake for 12 minutes until golden and crisp. Transfer to a wire rack to cool and serve.

CHOCOLATE & GINGER FLORENTINES

❦

Makes 14–16

40 g/1^{1}/$_{2}$ oz butter
5 tbsp double cream
50 g/2 oz caster sugar
65 g/2^{1}/$_{2}$ oz chopped almonds
25 g/1 oz flaked almonds
40 g/1^{1}/$_{2}$ oz glacé ginger, chopped
25 g/1 oz plain flour
pinch salt
150 g/5 oz dark chocolate

Preheat the oven to 180°C/350°F/Gas Mark 4, 10 minutes before baking. Lightly oil several baking sheets. Melt the butter, cream and sugar together in a saucepan and bring slowly to the boil. Remove from the heat and stir in the almonds and the glacé ginger.

Leave to cool slightly, then mix in the flour and the salt. Blend together, then place heaped teaspoons of the mixture on the baking sheets. Make sure they are spaced well apart, as they expand during cooking. Flatten them slightly with the back of a wet spoon.

Bake in the preheated oven for 10–12 minutes until just brown at the edges. Leave to cool slightly. Using a spatula, carefully transfer the Florentines to a wire rack and leave to cool.

Melt the chocolate in a heatproof bowl set over a saucepan of gently simmering water. Alternatively, melt the chocolate in the microwave, according to the manufacturer's instructions, until just liquid and smooth. Spread thickly over one side of the Florentines, then mark wavy lines through the chocolate using a fork and leave until firm.

CLASSIC FLAPJACKS

❦

Makes 12

175 g/6 oz butter, plus extra
for greasing
125 g/4 oz demerara sugar
2 tbsp golden syrup
175 g/6 oz jumbo porridge oats
few drops vanilla extract

Preheat the oven to 160°C/325°F/Gas Mark 3. Butter a
20.5 cm/8 inch square baking tin.

Place the butter, sugar and golden syrup in a saucepan
and heat gently until the butter has melted and every
grain of sugar has dissolved.

Remove from the heat and stir in the oats and vanilla
extract. Stir well and then spoon the mixture into the
prepared tin.

Smooth level with the back of a large spoon. Bake in the
centre of the oven for 30–40 minutes until golden. Leave
to cool in the tin for 10 minutes, then mark into fingers
and leave in the tin until completely cold. When cold, cut
into fingers with a sharp knife.

CHOCOLATE ORANGE BISCUITS

Makes 30

100 g/3¹/₂ oz dark chocolate
125 g/4 oz butter
125 g/4 oz caster sugar
pinch salt
1 medium egg, beaten
grated zest of 2 oranges
200 g/7 oz plain flour
1 tsp baking powder
125 g/4 oz icing sugar
1–2 tbsp orange juice

Preheat the oven to 200°C/400°F/Gas Mark 6, 15 minutes before baking. Lightly oil several baking sheets. Coarsely grate the chocolate and reserve. Beat the butter and sugar together until creamy. Add the salt, beaten egg and half the orange zest and beat again.

Sift the flour and baking powder, add to the bowl with the grated chocolate and beat to form a dough. Shape into a ball, wrap in clingfilm and chill in the refrigerator for 2 hours.

Roll the dough out on a lightly floured surface to 5 mm/¼ inch thickness and cut into 5 cm/2 inch rounds. Place the rounds on the prepared baking sheets, allowing room for expansion. Bake in the preheated oven for 10–12 minutes until firm. Remove the biscuits from the oven and leave to cool slightly. Using a spatula, transfer to a wire rack and leave to cool.

Sift the icing sugar into a small bowl and stir in sufficient orange juice to make a smooth, spreadable icing. Pipe or spread the icing over the biscuits, leave until almost set, then sprinkle on the remaining grated orange zest before serving.

CHOCOLATE MACAROONS

❦

Makes 20

65 g/2½ oz dark chocolate
125 g/4 oz ground almonds
125 g/4 oz caster sugar
¼ tsp almond extract
1 tbsp cocoa powder
2 medium egg whites
1 tbsp icing sugar

Preheat the oven to 180°C/350°F/Gas Mark 4, 10 minutes before baking. Lightly oil several baking sheets and line with sheets of nonstick baking parchment. Melt the chocolate in a heatproof bowl set over a saucepan of simmering water. Alternatively, melt in the microwave, according to the manufacturer's instructions. Stir until smooth, then cool slightly.

Place the ground almonds in a food processor and add the sugar, almond extract, cocoa powder and 1 of the egg whites. Add the melted chocolate and a little of the other egg white and blend to make a soft, smooth paste. Alternatively, place the ground almonds with the sugar, almond extract and cocoa powder in a bowl and make a well in the centre. Add the melted chocolate with sufficient egg white and gradually blend together to form a smooth but not sticky paste.

Shape the dough into small balls the size of large walnuts and place them on the prepared baking sheets. Flatten them slightly, then brush with a little water. Sprinkle over a little icing sugar and bake in the preheated oven for 10–12 minutes until just firm.

Using a spatula, carefully lift the macaroons off the baking parchment and transfer to a wire rack to cool. These are best served immediately, but can be stored in an airtight container.

SWEET PIES

& PUDDINGS

No meal is complete without a dessert and, here, we have a tempting selection of baked puddings and delicious pastry desserts and pies. Again, every baker should know the classics, such as Apple Pie, Rhubarb and Raspberry Cobbler, Lemon Meringue Pie and cheesecake, but then there are so many other delights to try, such as the Banoffee Pie or chocolate versions of classics, such as Chocolate Lemon Tartlets and the decadent Chocolate Pecan Angel Pie.

APPLE PIE

Serves 6–8

175 g/6 oz plain flour
pinch salt
40 g/1¹/₂ oz lard or white
vegetable fat
40 g/1¹/₂ oz butter or block
margarine
1 tbsp caster sugar

For the filling:

500 g/1¹/₄ lb cooking apples,
peeled, cored and sliced
125 g/4 oz caster sugar
1 tsp ground cinnamon
½ tsp ground nutmeg
50 g/2 oz sultanas
15 g/¹/₂ oz butter
milk, for glazing
caster sugar, for sprinkling

Sift the flour and salt into a bowl or a food processor and add the fats, cut into small pieces. Rub in with your fingertips, or process, until the mixture resembles fine crumbs. Mix in the sugar and add 2–3 tablespoons cold water to form a soft dough, then knead lightly until smooth. Wrap and chill for 30 minutes.

Preheat the oven to 220°C/425°F/Gas Mark 7 and grease a 1.2 litre/ 2¹/₄ pint deep pie dish. Roll out the pastry on a lightly floured surface. Turn the pie dish upside down onto the pastry and cut round it to form the lid. Roll the trimmings into a 2.5 cm/1 inch strip and press this firmly onto the top edge of the dish.

Mix the sliced apples with the sugar, spices and sultanas. Place in the dish and then dot with butter. Dampen the pastry edge with water, then place the pastry lid over. Press the edges to seal, and flute together with your thumb and forefinger. Make a hole in the centre to allow the steam to escape, then decorate with pastry trimmings.

Brush with milk, then sprinkle with caster sugar. Bake for 10 minutes, then turn the oven temperature down to 190°C/350°F/Gas Mark 5 and bake for a further 25–30 minutes until crisp and golden. Serve hot straight away with cream or custard.

RHUBARB & RASPBERRY COBBLER

❀

Serves 4

325 g/11½ oz rhubarb, cut
into chunks
175 g/6 oz raspberries
50 g/2 oz golden caster sugar
zest and juice of 1 orange

For the topping:

225 g/8 oz plain flour
1 tbsp baking powder
50 g/2 oz butter, diced
50 g/2 oz caster sugar
150 ml/¼ pint milk
custard or double cream,
to serve

Preheat the oven to 220°C/425°F/Gas Mark 7. Butter a 1.7 litre/3 pint ovenproof dish.

Mix the rhubarb chunks with the raspberries and sugar and place in the buttered dish. Finely grate the zest from the orange and set aside. Squeeze out the juice and add to the dish with the rhubarb. Cover the dish with a piece of foil and bake for 20 minutes.

To make the topping, sift the flour and baking powder into a bowl and stir in the grated orange zest. Rub in the butter with your fingertips until the mixture resembles fine crumbs. Stir in the caster sugar and quickly add the milk. Mix with a fork to make a soft dough. (The mixture has to be made quickly as the raising agent – baking powder – starts to activate as soon as liquid is added.)

Take the dish out of the oven and discard the foil. Break off rough tablespoons of the dough and drop them on top of the fruit filling. Bake for about 25 minutes until the topping is firm and golden. Serve immediately with custard or single cream.

LEMON MERINGUE PIE

❦

Serves 4–6

175 g/6 oz plain flour
pinch salt
40 g/1¹/₂ oz lard or white vegetable fat
40 g/1¹/₂ oz butter or
block margarine

For the filling:

grated zest and juice of 2 lemons
75 g/3 oz granulated sugar
300 ml/¹/₂ pint water
40 g/1¹/₂ oz cornflour
2 large egg yolks

For the topping:

2 large egg whites
125 g/4 oz caster sugar

Preheat the oven to 200°C/400°F/Gas Mark 6 and place a baking sheet in the oven to heat. Sift the flour and salt into a bowl or a food processor and add the fats, cut into small pieces. Rub in with your fingertips, or process, until the mixture resembles fine crumbs. Mix in 2–3 tablespoons cold water to form a soft dough, then knead lightly until smooth. Grease a 20.5 cm/8 inch round flan tin. Roll out the pastry on a lightly floured surface and use to line the dish. Chill for 30 minutes while you make the filling.

Put the zest and granulated sugar in a pan with 300 ml/¹/₂ pint water in a heavy-based pan over a low heat and stir until the sugar has dissolved. Blend the cornflour with the lemon juice to a smooth paste, then add to the pan and bring to the boil, stirring all the time. Boil for 2 minutes, then remove from the heat and beat in the egg yolks. Set aside to cool.

Prick the pastry case, line with greaseproof paper and pour in baking beans. Place on the baking sheet and bake for 10 minutes. Remove from the oven and remove the paper and beans. Bake the pastry for a further 10 minutes. Remove from the oven, spoon the lemon filling into the pastry case and set aside. Reduce the temperature to 150°C/300°F/Gas Mark 2. Whisk the egg whites in a clean, dry bowl until very stiff. Whisk in half the caster sugar a little at a time, then fold in the remainder. Spread over the lemon filling, making sure it covers the top, right to the edges of the filling. Bake for 30 minutes until the meringue is golden. Leave to 'settle' for 20 minutes before serving, or eat cold on the day of baking.

CLASSIC APPLE STRUDEL

❧

Serves 8

700 g/1¹/₂ lb cooking apples
zest and juice of 1 orange
50 g/2 oz natural caster sugar
75 g/3 oz raisins
125 g/4 oz butter
50 g/2 oz fresh white breadcrumbs
40 g/1¹/₂ oz flaked almonds
¹/₂ tsp ground cinnamon
350 g/12 oz filo pastry sheets
icing sugar, for dusting
whipped cream, crème fraîche or
natural yogurt, to serve

Preheat the oven to 190°C/375°F/Gas Mark 5 and butter a large baking sheet. Peel, core and slice the apples, finely grate the zest from the orange and squeeze out the juice. Place the apples, orange zest and juice and caster sugar in a pan and cook over a gentle heat for 10 minutes until the apples are tender, then pour into a bowl, stir in the raisins and leave to cool.

Melt 25 g/1 oz of the butter in a nonstick frying pan and add the breadcrumbs. Cook for a minute to brown, then add the almonds and cook for a further minute. Remove from the heat, stir in the cinnamon and leave to cool.

Melt the remaining butter and brush 1 large or 2 small filo sheets overlapping. Reserve 1 sheet for decoration and continue buttering and layering the sheets. Brush the top sheet with butter. Sprinkle over half the breadcrumb mixture, leaving a 5 cm/2 inch border. Top with the cooked apples, then the remaining breadcrumb mixture. Fold in the sides, then roll up to encase the filling. Place on the greased baking sheet seam-side down. Arrange the reserved sheet on top in ruffles and brush the roll all over with butter. Bake for 20–30 minutes until crisp and light golden. Place on a serving dish and dust with icing sugar. Serve sliced with whipped cream, crème fraîche or thick natural yogurt.

BANOFFEE PIE

Serves 6–8

175 g/6 oz plain flour
pinch salt
1 tbsp caster sugar
75 g/3 oz butter, diced
1 egg yolk

For the filling and topping:

75 g/3 oz butter
50 g/2 oz soft light brown sugar
225 g/8 oz canned condensed milk
2 tbsp milk
3 bananas, peeled and sliced
150 ml/¼ pint double cream
25 g/1 oz plain chocolate, grated,
to decorate

Sift the flour and salt into a bowl or a food processor and add the sugar and butter. Rub in, or process, until the mixture resembles fine crumbs. Add the egg yolk and a few drops of cold water and mix to a dough. Knead until smooth, then wrap in clingfilm and chill for 30 minutes.

Preheat the oven to 200°C/400°F/Gas Mark 6 and grease a 20.5 cm/ 8 inch round flan tin. Roll the pastry out on a lightly floured surface and use to line the tin. Press the pastry into the sides of the tin and prick the base with a fork. Line the pastry case with greaseproof paper and baking beans, bake for 10 minutes, remove the beans, then bake for a further 5–10 minutes until golden. Place the tin on a wire rack to cool.

Meanwhile, make the filling. Gently heat the butter and sugar in a small pan until the butter melts and all the grains of sugar dissolve. Bring to the boil, then let boil for 1 minute. Remove from the heat and add the condensed milk and the 2 tablespoons milk. Stir together, then bring back to the boil and let boil for 2 minutes, stirring constantly. Remove from the heat. Place the sliced bananas in the pastry case and pour the warm toffee over. Leave to cool for 1 hour. Whip the cream and spread over the cold banoffee filling. Sprinkle with the grated chocolate and serve immediately.

RICOTTA CHEESECAKE WITH STRAWBERRY COULIS

❀

Serves 6–8

125 g/4 oz digestive biscuits
100 g/3½ oz candied
peel, chopped
65 g/2½ oz butter, melted
150 ml/¼ pint crème fraîche
575 g/1¼ lb ricotta cheese
100 g/3½ oz caster sugar
seeds of 1 vanilla pod
2 large eggs
225 g/8 oz strawberries
25–50 g/1–2 oz caster sugar,
to taste
zest and juice of 1 orange

Preheat the oven to 170°C/325°F/Gas Mark 3. Line a 20.5 cm/8 inch springform tin with baking parchment. Place the biscuits into a food processor together with the peel. Blend until the biscuits are crushed and the peel is chopped. Add 50 g/2 oz of the melted butter and process until mixed. Tip into the tin and spread evenly over the bottom. Press firmly into place and reserve.

Blend together the crème fraîche, ricotta cheese, sugar, vanilla seeds and eggs in a food processor. With the motor running, add the remaining melted butter and blend for a few seconds. Pour the mixture onto the base. Transfer to the preheated oven and cook for about 1 hour, until set and risen round the edges, but slightly wobbly in the centre. Switch off the oven and allow to cool there. Chill in the refrigerator for at least 8 hours, or preferably overnight.

Wash and drain the strawberries. Hull the fruit and remove any soft spots. Put into the food processor, along with 25 g/1 oz of the sugar and the orange juice and zest. Blend until smooth. Add the remaining sugar to taste. Pass through a sieve to remove seeds and chill in the refrigerator until needed.

Cut the cheesecake into wedges, spoon over some of the strawberry coulis and serve.

MINI STRAWBERRY TARTLETS

❦

Makes 12 tartlets

225 g/8 oz plain flour
25 g/1 oz icing sugar
125 g/4 oz butter, diced
25 g/1 oz ground almonds
1 egg yolk

For the filling:

85 ml/3 fl oz double cream
175 g/6 oz full-fat cream cheese
25 g/1 oz vanilla caster sugar
2 tbsp amaretto almond-flavoured liqueur
250 g/9 oz strawberries, hulled, and halved if large
2 tbsp sieved raspberry jam
small mint leaves, to decorate

Sift the flour and icing sugar into a bowl and add the diced butter. Rub the butter into the flour with your fingertips until the mixture resembles fine crumbs. Alternatively, place the flour, icing sugar and butter in a food processor and process until fine crumbs form. Stir in the ground almonds and egg yolk and mix with 1 tablespoon cold water to form a soft dough. Cover with clingfilm and chill for 30 minutes.

Preheat the oven to 200°C/400°F/Gas Mark 6 and grease a 12-hole muffin tin. Roll out the dough on a lightly floured surface to 6 mm/$1/4$ inch thickness and cut out twelve 10 cm/4 inch circles. Press the circles into the holes in the tin, loosely fluting up the edges. Prick the bases with a fork and bake for 12–15 minutes until light golden. Leave to cool in the tins for 3 minutes, then remove to cool completely on a wire rack.

To make the filling, whip the cream until stiff then mix with the cream cheese, sugar and liqueur. Chill until needed and then spoon into the pastry cases.

Arrange the fresh strawberries on top and brush lightly with a little jam to glaze. Decorate with small fresh mint leaves and serve immediately.

GOATS' CHEESE & LEMON TART

Serves 8–10

For the pastry:

125 g/4 oz butter, cut into small pieces
225 g/8 oz plain flour
pinch salt
50 g/2 oz caster sugar
1 medium egg yolk

For the filling:

350 g/12 oz mild fresh goats' cheese, such as Chavroux
3 medium eggs, beaten
150 g/5 oz caster sugar
grated zest and juice of 3 lemons
450 ml/³/₄ pint double cream
fresh raspberries, to decorate and serve

Preheat the oven to 200°C/400°F/Gas Mark 6, 15 minutes before cooking. Rub the butter into the plain flour and salt until the mixture resembles breadcrumbs, then stir in the sugar. Beat the egg yolk with 2 tablespoons of cold water and add to the mixture. Mix together until a dough is formed, then turn the dough out onto a lightly floured surface and knead until smooth. Chill in the refrigerator for 30 minutes.

Roll the dough out thinly on a lightly floured surface and use to line a 4 cm/1¹/₂ inch deep 23 cm/9 inch fluted flan tin. Chill in the refrigerator for 10 minutes. Line the pastry case with greaseproof paper and baking beans or foil and bake blind in the preheated oven for 10 minutes. Remove the paper and beans or foil. Return to the oven for a further 12–15 minutes until cooked, then remove from the oven and leave to cool slightly. Reduce the oven temperature to 150°C/300°F/Gas Mark 2.

Beat the goats' cheese until smooth. Whisk in the eggs, sugar, lemon zest and juice. Add the cream and mix well.

Carefully pour the cheese mixture into the pastry case and return to the oven. Bake in the oven for 35–40 minutes until just set. If it begins to brown or swell, open the oven door for 2 minutes, then reduce the temperature to 120°C/250°F/Gas Mark ¹/₂ and leave the tart to cool in the oven. Chill in the refrigerator until cold. Decorate and serve with fresh raspberries.

AUTUMN TART

⟨✿⟩

Serves 6–8

175 g/6 oz plain flour
pinch salt
1 tbsp caster sugar
75 g/3 oz butter, diced
1 egg yolk

For the filling:

50 g/2 oz butter
50 g/2 oz caster sugar
50 g/2 oz ground almonds
1 egg yolk
2 dessert apples, peeled, cored
and sliced
4 plums, pitted and sliced
2 tbsp lemon juice
2 tbsp caster sugar
milk, for brushing
crème fraîche, to serve

Sift the flour and salt into a bowl or a food processor, add the sugar and butter and rub in or process until the mixture resembles fine crumbs. Add the egg yolk and 1 tablespoon cold water and mix to a dough. Knead until smooth, then wrap in clingfilm and chill for 30 minutes.

Preheat the oven to 180°C/350°F/Gas Mark 4 and grease a 20.5 cm/ 8 inch round flan tin. Roll the pastry out on a lightly floured surface and use to line the tin. Trim the top and reserve the trimmings. Press the pastry into the sides of the tin and prick the base with a fork.

To make the filling, put the butter and sugar in a bowl and beat until fluffy. Beat in the ground almonds and egg yolk and spoon into the pastry case. Arrange the sliced fruit over the filling. Mix the lemon juice and caster sugar together and brush over the top of the fruit filling.

Roll out the pastry trimmings and cut out leaf shapes and mark veins on. Brush the edge of the tart with milk, place the leaves round the edge and brush with milk. Bake for 30 minutes, or until the pastry is golden and the fruit is tender and golden. Serve with crème fraîche.

LATTICE TREACLE TART

Serves 4

For the pastry:

175 g/6 oz plain flour
40 g/1¹/2 oz butter
40 g/1¹/2 oz white vegetable fat

For the filling:

225 g/8 oz golden syrup
finely grated zest and juice
of 1 lemon
75 g/3 oz fresh white breadcrumbs
1 small egg, beaten

Preheat the oven to 190°C/375°F/Gas Mark 5. Make the pastry by placing the flour, butter and white vegetable fat in a food processor. Blend in short sharp bursts until the mixture resembles fine breadcrumbs. Remove from the processor and place on a pastry board or in a large bowl.

Stir in enough cold water to make a dough and knead in a large bowl or on a floured surface until smooth and pliable.

Roll out the pastry and use to line a 20.5 cm/8 inch loose-bottomed fluted flan dish or tin. Reserve the pastry trimmings for decoration. Chill for 30 minutes.

Meanwhile, to make the filling, place the golden syrup in a saucepan and warm gently with the lemon zest and juice. Tip the breadcrumbs into the pastry case and pour the syrup mixture over the top.

Roll the pastry trimmings out on a lightly floured surface and cut into 6–8 thin strips. Lightly dampen the pastry edge of the tart, then place the strips across the filling in a lattice pattern. Brush the ends of the strips with water and seal to the edge of the tart. Brush a little beaten egg over the pastry and bake in the preheated oven for 25 minutes, or until the filling is just set. Serve hot or cold.

ICED BAKEWELL TART

∽◯◯◯∾

Cuts into 8 slices

For the rich pastry:

175 g/6 oz plain flour
pinch salt
65 g/2½ oz butter, cut into pieces
50 g/2 oz white vegetable fat,
cut into small pieces
2 small egg yolks, beaten

For the filling:

125 g/4 oz butter, melted
125 g/4 oz caster sugar
125 g/4 oz ground almonds
2 large eggs, beaten
few drops almond extract
2 tbsp seedless raspberry jam

For the icing:

125 g/4 oz icing sugar, sifted
6–8 tsp fresh lemon juice
25 g/1 oz toasted flaked almonds

Preheat the oven to 200°C/400°F/Gas Mark 6. Place the flour and salt in a bowl and rub in the butter and vegetable fat until the mixture resembles breadcrumbs. Alternatively, blend quickly, in short bursts in a food processor.

Add the eggs with sufficient water to make a soft, pliable dough. Knead lightly on a floured board, then chill in the refrigerator for about 30 minutes. Roll out the pastry and use to line a 23 cm/9 inch loose-bottomed flan tin.

For the filling, mix together the melted butter, sugar, almonds and beaten eggs and add a few drops of almond extract. Spread the base of the pastry case with the raspberry jam and spoon the egg mixture over the top. Bake in the preheated oven for about 30 minutes until the filling is firm and golden brown. Remove from the oven and allow to cool completely.

When the tart is cold make the icing by mixing together the icing sugar and lemon juice, a little at a time, until the icing is smooth and of a spreadable consistency. Spread the icing over the tart, leave to set for 2–3 minutes and sprinkle with the almonds. Chill in the refrigerator for about 10 minutes before serving.

CHOCOLATE LEMON TARTLETS

꧁꧂

Makes 10

1 quantity chocolate shortcrust pastry
(*see* page 25)
175 ml/6 fl oz double cream
175 g/6 oz dark chocolate, chopped
2 tbsp butter, diced
1 tsp vanilla essence/extract
350 g/12 oz lemon curd
225 ml/8 fl oz ready-made custard
225 ml/8 fl oz single cream
$1/2$ –1 tsp almond extract

To decorate:

grated chocolate
toasted flaked almonds

Preheat the oven to 200°C/400°F/Gas Mark 6, 15 minutes before baking. Roll the prepared pastry out on a lightly floured surface and use to line 10 x 7.5 cm/3 inch tartlet tins. Place a small piece of crumpled foil in each and bake blind in the preheated oven for 12 minutes. Remove from the oven and leave to cool.

Bring the cream to the boil, then remove from the heat and add the chocolate all at once. Stir until smooth and melted. Beat in the butter and vanilla extract and pour into the tartlets and leave to cool.

Beat the lemon curd until soft and spoon a thick layer over the chocolate in each tartlet, spreading gently to the edges. Do not chill in the refrigerator or the chocolate will be too firm.

Place the prepared custard sauce into a large bowl and gradually whisk in the cream and almond extract until the custard is smooth and runny.

To serve, spoon a little custard onto a plate and place a tartlet in the centre. Sprinkle with grated chocolate and almonds, then serve.

CHOCOLATE PECAN ANGEL PIE

Cuts into 8–10 slices

4 large egg whites
$^{1}/_{4}$ tsp cream of tartar
225 g/8 oz caster sugar
3 tsp vanilla extract
100 g/3$^{1}/_{2}$ oz pecans, lightly
toasted and chopped
75 g/3 oz dark chocolate chips
150 ml/$^{1}/_{4}$ pint double cream
150 g/5 oz white chocolate, grated

To decorate:

fresh raspberries
dark chocolate curls
few fresh mint sprigs

Preheat the oven to 110°C/225°F/Gas Mark $^{1}/_{4}$, 5 minutes before baking. Lightly oil a 23 cm/9 inch pie plate. Using an electric mixer, whisk the egg whites and cream of tartar on a low speed until foamy, then increase the speed and beat until soft peaks form. Gradually beat in the sugar, 1 tablespoon at a time, beating well after each addition, until stiff glossy peaks form and the sugar is completely dissolved. (Test by rubbing a bit of meringue between your fingers – if gritty, continue beating.) This will take about 15 minutes. Beat in 2 teaspoons of the vanilla extract, then fold in the nuts and the chocolate chips.

Spread the meringue evenly in the pie plate, making a shallow well in the centre and slightly building up the sides. Bake in the preheated oven for 1–1$^{1}/_{4}$ hours until a golden creamy colour. Lower the oven temperature if the meringue colours too quickly. Turn the oven off, but do not remove the meringue. Leave the oven door ajar (about 5 cm/2 inches) for about 1 hour. Transfer to a wire rack until cold.

Pour the double cream into a small saucepan and bring to the boil. Remove from the heat, add the grated white chocolate and stir until melted. Add the remaining vanilla extract and leave to cool, then whip until thick. Spoon the white chocolate cream into the pie shell, piling it high and swirling. Decorate with the raspberries and chocolate curls. Chill in the refrigerator for 2 hours before serving. To serve, add sprigs of mint and cut into slices.

BREAD & BUTTER PUDDING

Serves 4–6

2–3 tbsp unsalted butter, softened
4–6 slices white bread
75 g/3 oz mixed dried fruits
25 g/1 oz caster sugar, plus extra
for sprinkling
2 medium eggs
450 ml/³/₄ pint semi-skimmed
milk, warmed
freshly grated nutmeg
freshly made custard, to serve

Preheat the oven to 180°C/350°F/Gas Mark 4, 10 minutes before cooking. Lightly butter a 1.1 litre/2 pint ovenproof dish. Butter the bread and cut into quarters. Arrange half the bread in the dish and scatter over two-thirds of the dried fruit and sugar. Repeat the layering, finishing with the dried fruits.

Beat the eggs and milk together and pour over the bread and butter. Leave to stand for 30 minutes.

Sprinkle with the remaining sugar and a little nutmeg and carefully place in the oven. Cook for 40 minutes, or until the pudding has lightly set and the top is golden.

Remove and sprinkle with a little extra sugar, if liked. Serve with freshly made custard.

LUXURY MINCE PIES

Makes 20

275 g/10 oz plain flour
25 g/1 oz ground almonds
175 g/6 oz butter, diced
75 g/3 oz icing sugar
zest of 1 lemon, finely grated
1 egg yolk
3 tbsp milk

For the filling:

225 g/8 oz mincemeat
1 tbsp dark rum or orange juice
zest of 1 orange, finely grated
75 g/3 oz dried cranberries
icing sugar, for dusting

Sift the flour and ground almonds into a bowl or a food processor and add the butter. Rub in, or process, until the mixture resembles fine crumbs. Sift in the icing sugar and stir in the lemon zest. Whisk the egg yolk and milk together in a separate bowl and stir into the mixture until a soft dough forms. Wrap the pastry in clingfilm and chill for 30 minutes.

Preheat the oven to 200°C/400°F/Gas Mark 6. Grease two 12-hole patty tins. Roll out the pastry on a lightly floured surface to 3 mm/$^1/_8$ inch thickness. Cut out 20 rounds using a 7.5 cm/3 inch fluted round pastry cutter. Re-roll the trimmings into thin strips.

Mix the filling ingredients together in a bowl. Place 1 tablespoon of the filling in each pastry case, then dampen the edges of each case with a little water. Put four strips of pastry over the top of each case to form a lattice.

Bake for 10–15 minutes until the pastry is crisp. Dust with icing sugar and serve hot or cold.

BAKED APPLE DUMPLINGS

Serves 4

225 g/8 oz self-raising flour
$1/4$ tsp salt
125 g/4 oz shredded suet
4 medium cooking apples
4–6 tsp luxury mincemeat
1 medium egg white, beaten
2 tsp caster sugar
custard or vanilla sauce,
to serve

Preheat the oven to 200°C/400°F/Gas Mark 6. Lightly oil a baking tray. Place the flour and salt in a bowl and stir in the suet. Add just enough water to the mixture to mix to a soft but not sticky dough, using the fingertips.

Turn the dough onto a lightly floured board and knead lightly into a ball. Divide the dough into 4 pieces and roll out each piece into a thin square, large enough to encase the apples.

Peel and core the apples and place 1 apple in the centre of each square of pastry. Fill the centre of the apple with mincemeat, brush the edges of each pastry square with water and draw the corners up to meet over each apple. Press the edges of the pastry firmly together and decorate with pastry leaves and shapes made from the extra pastry trimmings.

Place the apples on the prepared baking tray, brush with the egg white and sprinkle with the sugar. Bake in the preheated oven for 30 minutes, or until golden and the pastry and apples are cooked. Serve the dumplings hot with the custard or vanilla sauce.

FREEFORM FRUIT PIE

Serves 6

175 g/6 oz plain flour
40 g/1½ oz lard or white
vegetable fat
40 g/1½ oz butter
1 tbsp caster sugar
1 medium egg, separated

For the filling:

2 tbsp semolina
600 g/1¼ lb gooseberries
75 g/3 oz caster sugar
zest of 1 orange, finely grated
1 egg, separated
2 tbsp caster sugar
vanilla ice cream, to serve

Sift the flour into a bowl or a food processor and add the fats, cut into small pieces. Rub in with your fingertips, or process, until fine crumbs form. Stir in the sugar and the egg yolk and mix with a few drops of cold water to make a soft dough. Knead lightly, then wrap in clingfilm and chill for 30 minutes.

Preheat the oven to 190°C/375°F/Gas Mark 5 and grease a large baking sheet. Roll out the pastry to a circle approximately 30 cm/12 inches wide.

Lift the pastry onto a rolling pin and place on the baking sheet.

Beat the egg yolk and brush this lightly over the pastry. Sprinkle the semolina lightly over the egg yolk.

Mix the gooseberries with the sugar and zest and pile into the centre of the pastry circle, leaving a border of 8 cm/3¼ inches all round.

Gather the pastry edges up over the filling. Press the edges together roughly, leaving the centre exposed. Beat the egg whites until foaming, then brush over the pastry. Scatter over the caster sugar and bake for about 30 minutes until golden. Remove to a serving plate and serve with vanilla ice cream.

GOLDEN CASTLE PUDDING

Serves 4–6

125 g/4 oz butter
125 g/4 oz caster sugar
few drops vanilla extract
2 medium eggs, beaten
125 g/4 oz self-raising flour
4 tbsp golden syrup
crème fraîche or ready-made
custard, to serve

Preheat the oven to 180°C/350°F/Gas Mark 4. Lightly oil 4–6 individual pudding bowls and place a small circle of lightly oiled nonstick baking or greaseproof paper in the base of each.

Place the butter and caster sugar in a large bowl, then beat together until the mixture is pale and creamy. Stir in the vanilla extract and gradually add the beaten eggs, a little at a time. Add a tablespoon of flour after each addition of egg and beat well.

When the mixture is smooth, add the remaining flour and fold in gently. Add a tablespoon of water and mix to form a soft mixture that will drop easily off a spoon.

Spoon enough mixture into each basin to come halfway up the tin, allowing enough space for the puddings to rise. Place on a baking sheet and bake in the preheated oven for about 25 minutes until firm and golden brown.

Allow the puddings to stand for 5 minutes. Discard the paper circles and turn out onto individual serving plates.

Warm the golden syrup in a small saucepan and pour a little over each pudding. Serve hot with the crème fraîche or custard.

BREADS

& SCONES

There is nothing quite like the aroma of freshly made bread filling your kitchen, and nothing beats the satisfaction of tucking into your home-baked loaf. Start with a Quick Brown Bread or Classic White Loaf, then mix things up with Wholemeal Walnut Bread, or make some Tomato & Basil Rolls to have with dinner. Do not forget breads such as focaccia, chapatti and naan, to go with a world of dishes; and then there are the homely Hot Cross Buns and Traditional Oven Scones, or try our tea breads – perfect for that afternoon nibble with a cuppa!

QUICK BROWN BREAD

✦

Makes two 450 g/1 lb loaves

700 g/1¹/₂ lb strong wholemeal flour
2 tsp salt
¹/₂ tsp caster sugar
7 g oz sachet fast-action dried yeast
450 ml/³/₄ pint warm water

To finish:

beaten egg, to glaze
1 tbsp plain white flour, to dust

For onion and caraway seed rolls:

1 small onion, peeled and finely chopped
1 tbsp olive oil
2 tbsp caraway seeds
milk, to glaze

Preheat the oven to 200°C/400°F/Gas Mark 6, 15 minutes before baking. Oil two 450 g/1 lb loaf tins. Sift the flour, salt and sugar into a large bowl, adding the bran remaining in the sieve. Stir in the yeast, then make a well in the centre.

Pour the warm water into the dry ingredients and mix to form a soft dough, adding a little more water if needed. Knead on a lightly floured surface for 10 minutes, or until smooth and elastic. Divide in half, shape into two oblongs and place in the tins. Cover with oiled clingfilm and leave in a warm place for 40 minutes, or until risen to the tops of the tins.

Glaze one loaf with the beaten egg and dust the other loaf generously with the plain flour. Bake the loaves in the preheated oven for 35 minutes, or until well risen and lightly browned. Turn out of the tins and return to the oven for 5 minutes to crisp the sides. Cool on a wire rack.

For the onion and caraway seed rolls, gently fry the onion in the oil until soft. Reserve until the onion is cool, then stir into the dry ingredients with 1 tablespoon of the caraway seeds. Make the dough as before. Divide the dough into 16 pieces and shape into rolls. Put on two oiled baking trays, cover with oiled clingfilm and prove for 30 minutes. Glaze the rolls with milk and sprinkle with the rest of the seeds. Bake for 25–30 minutes, cool on a wire rack and serve.

CLASSIC WHITE LOAF

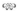

Makes one 900 g/2 lb loaf

700 g/1½ lb strong white flour
1 tbsp salt
25 g/1 oz butter, cubed
1 tsp caster sugar
2 tsp fast-action dried yeast
150 ml/¼ pint milk
300 ml/½ pint warm water
1 tbsp plain flour, to dredge

For a light wholemeal variation:

450 g/1 lb strong wholemeal flour
225 g/8 oz strong white flour
beaten egg, to glaze
1 tbsp kibbled wheat, to finish

Preheat the oven to 220°C/425°F/Gas Mark 7, 15 minutes before baking. Oil and line the base of a 900 g/2 lb loaf tin with greaseproof paper. Sift the flour and salt into a large bowl. Rub in the butter, then stir in the sugar and yeast. Make a well in the centre.

Add the milk and the warm water to the dry ingredients. Mix to a soft dough, adding a little more water if needed. Turn out the dough and knead on a lightly floured surface for 10 minutes, or until smooth and elastic.

Place the dough in an oiled bowl, cover with clingfilm or a clean tea towel and leave in a warm place to rise for 1 hour, or until doubled in size. Knead again for a minute or two to knock out the air. Shape the dough into an oblong and place in the prepared tin. Cover with oiled clingfilm and leave to rise for a further 30 minutes, or until the dough reaches the top of the tin. Dredge the top of the loaf with flour, or brush with the egg glaze and scatter with kibbled wheat if making the wholemeal version. Bake the loaf on the middle shelf of the preheated oven for 15 minutes.

Turn down the oven to 200°C/400°F/Gas Mark 6. Bake the loaf for a further 20–25 minutes until well risen and hollow-sounding when tapped underneath. Turn out, cool on a wire rack and serve.

MULTIGRAIN BREAD

✑

Makes 1 large loaf

350 g/12 oz strong white flour
2 tsp salt
225 g/8 oz strong granary flour
125 g/4 oz rye flour
25 g/1 oz butter, diced
2 tsp fast-action dried yeast
25 g/1 oz rolled oats
2 tbsp sunflower seeds
1 tbsp malt extract
450 ml/³/₄ pint warm water
1 medium egg, beaten

Preheat the oven to 220°C/425°F/Gas Mark 7, 15 minutes before baking. Sift the white flour and salt into a large bowl. Stir in the granary and rye flours, then rub in the butter until the mixture resembles breadcrumbs. Stir in the yeast, oats and seeds and make a well in the centre.

Stir the malt extract into the warm water until dissolved. Add the malt water to the dry ingredients. Mix to a soft dough. Turn the dough out onto a lightly floured surface and knead for 10 minutes, or until smooth and elastic.

Put in an oiled bowl, cover with clingfilm and leave to rise in a warm place for 1¹/₂ hours, or until doubled in size. Turn out and knead again for a minute or two to knock out the air. Shape into an oval loaf about 30.5 cm/12 inches long and place on a well-oiled baking sheet. Cover with oiled clingfilm and leave to rise for 40 minutes, or until doubled in size.

Brush the loaf with beaten egg and bake in the preheated oven for 35–45 minutes until the bread is well risen, browned and sounds hollow when the base is tapped. Leave to cool on a wire rack, then serve.

WHOLEMEAL WALNUT BREAD

❧

Makes two 350 g/ 12 oz loaves

700 g/1½ lb strong wholemeal
bread flour
1½ tsp sea salt
7 g sachet fast-action dried yeast
450 ml/¾ pint lukewarm water
2 tbsp walnut oil
1 tbsp clear honey
125 g/4 oz walnuts

Place the flour, salt and yeast in a large bowl and stir together. Make a well in the middle and pour in the lukewarm water, the walnut oil and the honey. Gradually work the flour into the liquid until it comes together to make a ball of dough.

Place the dough on a lightly floured surface and knead for about 10 minutes until it is smooth, soft and stretchy, or place the dough in a tabletop mixer fitted with a dough hook and knead for 5 minutes until smooth.

Preheat a grill and line a baking sheet with foil. Place the walnuts on the baking sheet and grill for a few minutes to toast them. Cool the nuts, then chop them coarsely. Knead the chopped walnuts into the dough. Divide the dough in half and then shape into two balls. Dust the top of the bread lightly with flour and cut slashes into the top with a sharp knife to a depth of about 2 cm/¾ inch. Oil a large baking sheet and place the dough on it. Cover with oiled clingfilm and leave in a warm place for about 40 minutes to 1 hour until doubled in size.

Preheat the oven to 200°C/400°F/Gas Mark 6. Discard the clingfilm and place the dough in the oven. Bake for 35 minutes until golden. Tap the bread, which should sound hollow when it is cooked. If it sounds heavy, bake it for a few more minutes. Place on a wire rack to cool.

IRISH SODA BREAD

❦

Makes 1 loaf

400 g/14 oz plain white flour, plus 1 tbsp for dusting
1 tsp salt
2 tsp bicarbonate of soda
15 g/^{1}/$_2$ oz butter
50 g/2 oz coarse oatmeal
1 tsp clear honey
300 ml/^{1}/$_2$ pint buttermilk
2 tbsp milk

For a wholemeal variation:

400 g/14 oz plain wholemeal flour, plus 1 tbsp for dusting
1 tbsp milk

Preheat the oven to 200°C/400°F/Gas Mark 6, 15 minutes before baking. Sift the flour, salt and bicarbonate of soda into a large bowl. Rub in the butter until the mixture resembles fine breadcrumbs. Stir in the oatmeal and make a well in the centre.

Mix the honey, buttermilk and milk together and add to the dry ingredients. Mix to a soft dough.

Knead the dough on a lightly floured surface for 2–3 minutes until the dough is smooth. Shape into a 20.5 cm/8 inch round and place on an oiled baking sheet.

Thickly dust the top of the bread with flour. Using a sharp knife, cut a deep cross on top, going about halfway through the loaf.

Bake on the middle shelf of the preheated oven for 30–35 minutes until the bread is slightly risen, golden and sounds hollow when tapped underneath. Cool on a wire rack. Eat on the day of making.

For a wholemeal soda bread, use all wholemeal flour instead of the white flour and add an extra tablespoon of milk when mixing together. Dust the top with wholemeal flour and bake.

TOMATO & BASIL ROLLS

Makes 10 large rolls

575 g/1¼ lb strong white bread flour
2 tsp salt
7 g sachet fast-action dried yeast
5 tbsp olive oil
300 ml/½ pint lukewarm water
2 tbsp tomato purée
100 g/3½ oz soft sun-dried
tomatoes, chopped
25 g/1 oz chopped fresh basil
25 g/1 oz Parmesan cheese,
finely grated
1 tbsp sea salt

Sift the flour and salt into a bowl and stir in the yeast. Add 4 tablespoons of the olive oil, the lukewarm water and the tomato purée and mix to a soft dough. Knead the dough by hand for 10 minutes, or place in a tabletop mixer fitted with a dough hook and knead for 5 minutes until smooth and elastic.

Return to the bowl and cover with oiled clingfilm. Leave in a warm place for about 1 hour until doubled in size. Turn the dough onto a floured surface and punch it to knock out all the air. Knead in the chopped tomatoes, basil and Parmesan cheese.

Cut the dough into 10 pieces. Roll each piece out into a ball and brush over the tops with the remaining 1 tablespoon olive oil. Make shallow diamond-shaped slashes across the top of each one with a sharp knife.

Cover the rolls with oiled clingfilm and leave for about 45 minutes until doubled in size. Preheat the oven to 220°C/425°F/Gas Mark 7, 10–15 minutes before baking. Discard the clingfilm and scatter the sea salt over the rolls. Bake for about 20 minutes until risen and golden and the rolls sound hollow when tapped. Leave to cool on a wire rack.

SWEET POTATO BAPS

❦

Makes 16

225 g/8 oz sweet potato
15 g/¹/₂ oz butter
freshly grated nutmeg
about 200 ml/7 fl oz milk
450 g/1 lb strong white flour
2 tsp salt
7 g sachet fast-action dried yeast
1 medium egg, beaten

To finish:

beaten egg, to glaze
1 tbsp rolled oats

Preheat the oven to 200°C/400°F/Gas Mark 6, 15 minutes before baking. Peel the sweet potato and cut into large chunks. Cook in a saucepan of boiling water for 12–15 minutes until tender. Drain well and mash with the butter and nutmeg. Stir in the milk, then leave until barely warm.

Sift the flour and salt into a large bowl. Stir in the yeast. Make a well in the centre. Add the mashed sweet potato and beaten egg and mix to a soft dough. Add a little more milk if needed, depending on the moisture in the sweet potato.

Turn out the dough onto a lightly floured surface and knead for about 10 minutes until smooth and elastic. Place in a lightly oiled bowl, cover with clingfilm and leave in a warm place to rise for about 1 hour until the dough doubles in size.

Turn out the dough and knead for a minute or two until smooth. Divide into 16 pieces, shape into rolls and place on a large oiled baking sheet. Cover with oiled clingfilm and leave to rise for 15 minutes.

Brush the rolls with beaten egg, then sprinkle half with rolled oats and leave the rest plain. Bake in the preheated oven for 12–15 minutes until well risen, lightly browned and sound hollow when the bases are tapped. Transfer to a wire rack and immediately cover with a clean tea towel to keep the crusts soft.

POPPY SEED PLAIT

❧

Makes 1 loaf

500 g/1 lb 2 oz strong white
bread flour
2 tsp salt
2 tsp caster sugar
25 g/1 oz white vegetable fat
7 g sachet fast-action dried yeast
150 ml /¹/₄ pint milk
150 ml/¹/₄ pint lukewarm water
1 medium egg, beaten
2 tbsp poppy seeds

Sift the flour and salt into a bowl and stir in the sugar. Cut the fat into small cubes and rub into the flour in the bowl until it forms fine crumbs. Stir in the yeast and add the milk and lukewarm water.

Mix to a soft dough. Place in a tabletop mixer fitted with a dough hook and knead for 5 minutes, or turn out onto a floured surface and knead by hand for about 10 minutes until smooth and elastic.

Return to the bowl and cover with oiled clingfilm. Leave in a warm place for about 1 hour until doubled in size. Discard the clingfilm, place the dough on a floured surface and knead it to knock out all the air.

Grease a baking sheet. Divide the dough into three equal pieces and roll each into a thin rope about 30 cm/12 inches long. Place the ropes side by side and plait them, starting from halfway down. Be careful not to stretch the dough. Join the ends and tuck underneath. Place the plaited loaf on the baking sheet. Cover with oiled clingfilm and leave to rise in a warm place for about 45 minutes until doubled in size.

Preheat the oven to 220°C/425°F/Gas Mark 7. Discard the clingfilm and brush the risen dough with the beaten egg. Sprinkle over the poppy seeds and bake for about 30 minutes or until golden. To test if the bread is cooked, tap the underside with your knuckles. It should sound hollow if the bread is done. Cool on a wire rack. Eat within 24 hours.

ROSEMARY &
OLIVE FOCACCIA

cℜ⁊

Makes 2 loaves

700 g/1¹/₂ lb strong white flour
pinch salt
pinch caster sugar
7 g/¹/₄ oz sachet fast-action
dried yeast
2 tsp freshly chopped rosemary
450 ml/³/₄ pint warm water
3 tbsp olive oil
75 g/3 oz pitted black olives,
roughly chopped
rosemary sprigs, to garnish

To finish:

3 tbsp olive oil
coarse sea salt
freshly ground black pepper

Preheat the oven to 200°C/400°F/Gas Mark 6, 15 minutes before baking. Sift the flour, salt and sugar into a large bowl. Stir in the yeast and rosemary. Make a well in the centre.

Pour in the warm water and the oil and mix to a soft dough. Turn onto a lightly floured surface and knead for about 10 minutes until smooth and elastic.

Pat the olives dry on kitchen paper, then gently knead into the dough. Put in an oiled bowl, cover with clingfilm and leave to rise in a warm place for 1¹/₂ hours, or until doubled in size.

Turn out the dough and knead again for a minute or two. Divide in half and roll out each piece to a 25.5 cm/10 inch round. Transfer to oiled baking sheets, cover with oiled clingfilm and leave to rise for 30 minutes.

Using the fingertips, make deep dimples all over the dough. Drizzle with the oil and sprinkle with sea salt.

Bake in the preheated oven for 20–25 minutes until risen and golden. Cool on a wire rack and garnish with sprigs of rosemary. Grind over a little black pepper before serving.

CHAPATTIS

❦

Makes 6

225 g/8 oz wholemeal flour
$^1/_2$ tsp salt
125 ml/4 fl oz warm water

Sift the flour and salt into a bowl, adding any bran left in the sieve. Add the water a little at a time and knead until a firm dough forms.

Replace the dough in the bowl and cover with a damp, clean cloth, such as a tea towel, and leave to rest for 20 minutes.

Divide the dough into 6 equal pieces and roll them out on a lightly floured surface into thin rounds about 15 cm/6 inches wide.

Preheat a heavy-based frying pan or a griddle pan until it is so hot that water will sizzle if a few drops are added.

Cook one chapatti at a time in the pan, pressing down until brown, then flip it over and cook it on the other side. Keep the breads warm, covered with a cloth, while you cook the remaining dough. Eat immediately, served with curry and rice.

SPICY FILLED NAAN BREAD

❦

Makes 6

400 g/14 oz strong white flour
1 tsp salt
1 tsp fast-action dried yeast
15 g/$\frac{1}{2}$ oz ghee or unsalted
butter, melted
1 tsp clear honey
200 ml/7 fl oz warm water

For the filling:

25 g/1 oz ghee or unsalted butter
1 small onion, peeled and
finely chopped
1 garlic clove, peeled and crushed
1 tsp ground coriander
1 tsp ground cumin
2 tsp grated fresh root ginger
pinch chilli powder
pinch ground cinnamon
salt and freshly ground
black pepper

Preheat the oven to 230°C/450°F/Gas Mark 8, 15 minutes before baking and place a large baking sheet in to heat up. Sift the flour and salt into a large bowl. Stir in the yeast and make a well in the centre. Add the ghee or melted butter, honey and the warm water. Mix to a soft dough.

Knead the dough on a lightly floured surface until smooth and elastic. Put in a lightly oiled bowl, cover with clingfilm and leave to rise for 1 hour, or until doubled in size.

For the filling, melt the ghee or butter in a frying pan and gently cook the onion for about 5 minutes. Stir in the garlic and spices and season to taste with salt and pepper. Cook for a further 6–7 minutes until soft. Remove from the heat, stir in 1 tablespoon of water and leave to cool.

Briefly knead the dough, then divide into six pieces. Roll out each piece of dough to 12.5 cm/5 inch rounds. Spoon the filling onto one half of each round. Fold over and press the edges together to seal. Re-roll to shape into flat ovals, about 16 cm/6$\frac{1}{2}$ inches long. Cover with oiled clingfilm and leave to rise for about 15 minutes.

Transfer the breads to the hot baking sheet and cook in the preheated oven for 10–12 minutes until puffed up and lightly browned. Serve hot.

HOT CROSS BUNS

❦

Makes 12

500 g/1 lb 2 oz strong white
bread flour
1 tsp salt
2 tsp mixed spice
50 g/2 oz soft light brown sugar
7 g sachet fast-action dried yeast
275 ml/9 fl oz milk
1 medium egg, beaten
50 g/2 oz butter, melted
and cooled
225 g/8 oz mixed dried fruit

For the decoration:

1 medium egg, beaten
75 g/3 oz shortcrust pastry
50 g/2 oz caster sugar

Sift the flour, salt and spice into a bowl and then stir in the sugar and yeast. In a jug, whisk together the milk and the egg. Add the liquid to the flour in the bowl with the cooled melted butter and mix to a soft dough. Knead for 10 minutes by hand, or for 5 minutes using a tabletop mixer fitted with a dough hook, until smooth and elastic.

Knead in the fruit and then place the dough in a bowl. Cover it with oiled clingfilm. Leave in a warm place for about 1 hour until doubled in size. Butter a large 32 x 23 cm/12 x 9 inch baking tray or a roasting tin. Cut the dough into 12 chunks and roll each one into a ball. Place in the tray, leaving enough space for the buns to rise and spread out. Cover with the oiled clingfilm and leave for about 45 minutes until doubled in size.

Preheat the oven to 200°C/400°F/Gas Mark 6. Discard the clingfilm and brush the buns with beaten egg. Roll the pastry into long thin strips. Place a pastry strip over and along the length of each bun, then place another strip in the opposite direction to make crosses. Repeat, topping all the buns with pastry crosses. Bake for 20–25 minutes until risen and golden.

Heat 2 tablespoons of water and add the caster sugar, continuing to heat gently until the sugar is completely dissolved. While still hot, turn the buns out of the tray and place on a wire rack. Brush the sugar glaze over the warm buns and leave to cool. These are best eaten on the day of baking. Split and toast any leftovers and serve with butter.

TRADITIONAL OVEN SCONES

Makes 8

225 g/8 oz self-raising flour
1 tsp baking powder
pinch salt
40 g/1¹/₂ oz butter, cubed
15 g/¹/₂ oz caster sugar
150 ml/¹/₄ pint milk, plus
1 tbsp for brushing
1 tbsp plain flour, to dust

For a lemon and sultana scone variation:

50 g/2 oz sultanas
finely grated zest of ¹/₂ lemon
beaten egg, to glaze

Preheat the oven to 220°C/425°F/Gas Mark 7, 15 minutes before baking. Sift the flour, baking powder and salt into a large bowl. Rub in the butter until the mixture resembles fine breadcrumbs. Stir in the sugar and mix in enough milk to give a fairly soft dough.

Knead the dough on a lightly floured surface for a few seconds until smooth. Roll out until 2 cm/¾ inch thick and stamp out 6.5 cm/ 2¹/₂ inch rounds with a floured plain cutter.

Place on an oiled baking sheet and brush the tops with milk (do not brush it over the sides or the scones will not rise properly). Dust with a little plain flour.

Bake in the preheated oven for 12–15 minutes until well risen and golden brown. Transfer to a wire rack and serve warm or leave to cool completely.

For lemon and sultana scones, stir in the sultanas and lemon zest with the sugar. Roll out until 2 cm/³/₄ inch thick and cut into 8 fingers, 10 x 2.5 cm/4 x 1 inch in size. Bake the scones as before.

CHEESE-CRUSTED POTATO SCONES

Makes 6

200 g/7 oz self-raising flour
25 g/1 oz wholemeal flour
1/2 tsp salt
1 1/2 tsp baking powder
25 g/1 oz butter, cubed
5 tbsp milk
175 g/6 oz cold mashed potato
freshly ground black pepper

To finish:

2 tbsp milk
40 g/1 1/2 oz mature Cheddar
cheese, finely grated
paprika, for dusting
basil sprig, to garnish

Preheat the oven to 220°C/425°F/Gas Mark 7, 15 minutes before baking. Sift the flours, salt and baking powder into a large bowl. Rub in the butter until the mixture resembles fine breadcrumbs.

Stir 4 tablespoons of the milk into the mashed potato and season with black pepper.

Add the dry ingredients to the potato mixture, mixing together with a fork and adding the remaining 1 tablespoon of milk if needed.

Knead the dough on a lightly floured surface for a few seconds until smooth. Roll out to a 15 cm/6 inch round and transfer to an oiled baking sheet. Mark the scone round into 6 wedges, cutting about halfway through with a small sharp knife. Brush with milk, then sprinkle with the cheese and a faint dusting of paprika. Bake on the middle shelf of the preheated oven for 15 minutes, or until well risen and golden brown.

Transfer to a wire rack and leave to cool for 5 minutes before breaking into wedges. Serve warm or leave to cool completely. Garnish with a sprig of basil and serve split and buttered.

BANANA & HONEY
TEA BREAD

❧

Makes one 900 g/2 lb loaf

2 large peeled bananas,
about 225 g/8 oz
1 tbsp fresh orange juice
125 g/4 oz soft margarine
125 g/4 oz soft light brown sugar
125 g/4 oz honey
2 medium eggs, beaten
225 g/8 oz wholemeal
self-raising flour
$1/2$ tsp ground cinnamon
75 g/3 oz sultanas

Preheat the oven to 180°C/350°F/Gas Mark 4. Grease a 900 g/2 lb loaf tin and line the base with a strip of nonstick baking parchment. Mash the bananas together in a large bowl with the orange juice.

Place the soft margarine, sugar and honey in the bowl and add the eggs. Sift in the flour and cinnamon, adding any bran left behind in the sieve. Beat everything together until light and fluffy and then fold in the sultanas.

Spoon the mixture into the prepared tin and smooth the top to make it level. Bake for about 1 hour until golden, well risen and a skewer inserted into the centre comes out clean.

Cool in the tin for 5 minutes, then turn out on a wire rack.

FRUITY APPLE TEA BREAD

✿

Cuts into 12 slices

125 g/4 oz butter
125 g/4 oz soft light brown sugar
275 g/10 oz sultanas
150 ml/^{1}/$_4$ pint apple juice
1 eating apple, peeled, cored and chopped
2 medium eggs, beaten
275 g/10 oz plain flour
^{1}/$_2$ tsp ground cinnamon
^{1}/$_2$ tsp ground ginger
2 tsp bicarbonate of soda
butter curls, to serve

To decorate:

1 eating apple, cored and sliced
1 tsp lemon juice
1 tbsp golden syrup, warmed

Preheat the oven to 180°C/350°F/Gas Mark 4. Oil and line the base of a 900 g/2 lb loaf tin with nonstick baking parchment.

Put the butter, sugar, sultanas and apple juice in a small saucepan. Heat gently, stirring occasionally, until the butter has melted. Tip into a mixing bowl and leave to cool.

Stir the chopped apple and beaten eggs into the cooled sultana mixture. Sift in the flour, spices and bicarbonate of soda and mix well.

Spoon into the prepared tin and level the top with the back of a spoon.

Toss the apple slices in lemon juice and arrange on top. Bake in the preheated oven for 50 minutes, then cover with foil to prevent the top from browning too much, and bake for a further 30–35 minutes until a skewer inserted into the centre comes out clean.

Brush the top with golden syrup then leave to cool in the tin before turning out onto a wire rack. Leave until cold. Remove the lining paper, cut into thick slices and serve with curls of butter.

SAVOURY

BAKING

Last but not least, we have got some savoury recipes for you to try your hand at – 'baking' does not just mean cakes! All ages will adore the essential Sausage Rolls and no baking book is complete without a Classic Quiche Lorraine. Have a go at making your own pizza – our spinach, pinenut and mascarpone variation is great! Or if you're after something a bit meatier, there are the classic Cornish Pasties and Beef & Red Wine Pie.

SAUSAGE ROLLS

❧

Makes 12

175 g/6 oz plain flour
pinch salt
40 g/1¹/₂ oz butter or
block margarine
40 g/1¹/₂ oz white vegetable fat
1 egg, beaten, to glaze

For the filling:

350 g/12 oz pork sausage meat
few drops Worcestershire sauce
salt and freshly ground
black pepper

Preheat the oven to 220°C/425°F/Gas Mark 7. Lightly oil two baking sheets.

Sift the flour and salt into a bowl. Cut the fats into small pieces and add them to the bowl. Rub the fats into the flour using your fingertips, or place the flour and fats in a food processor and process, until the mixture resembles fine crumbs.

Mix together with 1–2 tablespoons cold water to make a soft but not sticky dough. Knead lightly until smooth, then wrap in clingfilm and chill for 30 minutes.

Season the sausage meat with the Worcestershire sauce, salt and pepper. Divide into four, then roll each piece into a 25 cm/10 inch length. Roll out the pastry on a floured surface to a rectangle 40 x 25 cm/16 x 10 inches and cut into four strips 10 cm/4 inches wide. Place one roll of sausage meat down the centre of each pastry strip. Brush the edge of the pastry with beaten egg, fold each one over the meat and seal.

Brush the top and sides with beaten egg, then cut each large roll into 3. Cut slashes through the tops and place the 12 sausage rolls on the prepared baking sheets. Bake for 10 minutes, then reduce the temperature to 190°C/375°F/Gas Mark 5 and bake for a further 15 minutes, or until light golden. Eat hot or cold. Will keep for 2 days in an airtight container in the fridge.

BACON, MUSHROOM & CHEESE PUFFS

❦

Serves 4

1 tbsp olive oil
225 g/8 oz field mushrooms, wiped
and roughly chopped
225 g/8 oz rindless streaky bacon,
roughly chopped
2 tbsp freshly chopped parsley
salt and freshly ground
black pepper
350 g/12 oz ready-rolled puff pastry
sheets, thawed if frozen
25 g/1 oz Emmenthal cheese, grated
1 medium egg, beaten
salad leaves, such as rocket or
watercress, to garnish
tomatoes, to serve

Preheat the oven to 200°C/400°F/Gas Mark 6. Heat the olive oil in a large frying pan. Add the mushrooms and bacon and fry for 6–8 minutes until golden in colour. Stir in the parsley, season to taste with salt and pepper and allow to cool.

Roll the sheet of pastry a little thinner on a lightly floured surface to a 30 cm/12 inch square. Cut the pastry into 4 equal squares.

Stir the grated Emmenthal cheese into the mushroom mixture. Spoon a quarter of the mixture onto one half of each square.

Brush the edges of the square with a little of the beaten egg. Fold over the pastry to form a triangular parcel. Seal the edges well and place on a lightly oiled baking sheet. Repeat until the squares are done.

Make shallow slashes in the top of the pastry with a knife. Brush the parcels with the remaining beaten egg and cook in the preheated oven for 20 minutes, or until puffy and golden brown.

Serve warm or cold, garnished with the salad leaves and served with tomatoes.

CLASSIC QUICHE LORRAINE

❀

Serves 4–6

125 g/4 oz plain flour
pinch salt
25 g/1 oz white vegetable fat
25 g/1 oz butter

For the filling:

1 tsp vegetable oil
125 g/4 oz smoked streaky bacon,
trimmed and chopped
75 g/3 oz Gruyère cheese, grated
2 medium eggs, beaten
150 ml/^{1}/$_4$ pint single cream
1 tsp French mustard
tomatoes and green salad,
to serve

Sift the flour and salt into a bowl. Cut the fats into small pieces and rub into the flour with your fingertips until the mixture resembles fine crumbs. If you have a food processor, process the fats and flour until the mixture forms fine crumbs.

Stir in enough cold water, about 1 tbsp, to form a soft dough. Wrap the dough in clingfilm and chill for 30 minutes. Preheat the oven to 180°C/350°F/Gas Mark 4, 10 minutes before baking and grease a 20.5 cm/8 inch flan tin.

Roll out the pastry to a circle large enough to line the tin. Press into the tin and up the sides. Prick the base lightly with a fork. Line the pastry with a large piece of nonstick baking parchment. Pour in some baking beans. Place in the oven and bake for 15 minutes. Remove the tin from the oven and carefully lift out the paper and beans.

Pour the oil into a nonstick pan over a medium heat. Add the bacon and fry for about 4 minutes until crisp and brown, then leave to cool. Scatter the bacon into the pastry case with the grated cheese. Whisk the eggs with the cream and mustard and pour carefully into the pastry case. Bake for 30–35 minutes until golden and firm in the centre. Serve hot or cold with tomatoes and a green salad. To serve cold, keeps 24 hours refrigerated.

TOMATO & COURGETTE HERB TART

❦

Serves 4

4 tbsp olive oil
1 onion, peeled and finely chopped
3 garlic cloves, peeled and crushed
400 g/14 oz prepared puff pastry,
thawed if frozen
1 small egg, beaten
2 tbsp freshly chopped rosemary
2 tbsp freshly chopped parsley
175 g/6 oz rindless fresh soft
goats' cheese
4 ripe plum tomatoes, sliced
1 medium courgette, trimmed
and sliced
thyme sprigs, to garnish

Preheat the oven to 230°C/450°F/Gas Mark 8. Heat 2 tablespoons of the oil in a large frying pan. Fry the onion and garlic for about 4 minutes until softened and reserve.

Roll out the pastry on a lightly floured surface and cut out a 30 cm/12 inch circle. Brush the pastry with a little beaten egg, then prick all over with a fork. Transfer onto a dampened baking sheet and bake in the preheated oven for 10 minutes.

Turn the pastry over and brush with a little more egg. Bake for a further 5 minutes, then remove from the oven.

Mix together the onion, garlic and herbs with the goats' cheese and spread over the pastry.

Arrange the tomatoes and courgette over the goats' cheese and drizzle with the remaining oil.

Bake for 20–25 minutes until the pastry is golden brown and the topping is bubbling. Garnish with the thyme sprigs and serve immediately.

GARLIC WILD MUSHROOM GALETTES

❧

Serves 6

1 quantity quick flaky pastry
(*see* page 26), chilled
1 onion, peeled
1 red chilli, deseeded
2 garlic cloves, peeled
275 g/10 oz mixed mushrooms, e.g.
oyster, chestnut, morel, cep
and chanterelle
25 g/1 oz butter
2 tbsp freshly chopped parsley
125 g/4 oz mozzarella
cheese, sliced

To serve:

cherry tomatoes
mixed green salad leaves

Preheat the oven to 220°C/425°F/Gas Mark 7. On a lightly floured surface, roll out the chilled pastry very thinly. Cut out six 15 cm/6 inch circles and place on a lightly oiled baking sheet.

Thinly slice the onion, then divide into rings and reserve.

Thinly slice the chilli and slice the garlic into wafer-thin slivers. Add to the onions and reserve.

Wipe or lightly rinse the mushrooms. Halve or quarter any large mushrooms and keep the small ones whole.

Heat the butter in a frying pan and sauté the onion, chilli and garlic gently for about 3 minutes. Add the mushrooms and cook for about 5 minutes until beginning to soften. Stir the parsley into the mushroom mixture and drain off any excess liquid.

Pile the mushroom mixture onto the pastry circles within 5 mm/¼ inch of the edge. Arrange the sliced mozzarella cheese on top. Bake in the preheated oven for 12–15 minutes until golden brown and serve with the tomatoes and salad.

MEDITERRANEAN TARTLETS

❧

Makes 12

175 g/6 oz plain flour
pinch salt
75 g/3 oz butter or block margarine

For the filling:

50 g/2 oz feta cheese, crumbled
50 g/2 oz mozzarella
cheese, grated
2 spring onions, chopped
4 medium tomatoes, chopped,
seeds removed
2 tbsp chopped fresh basil
3 medium eggs
2 tbsp milk
salt and freshly ground
black pepper
green salad, to serve

Sift the flour and salt into a bowl. Cut the fat into small pieces and add to the bowl. Rub the fat into the flour using your fingertips, or place the flour and fat in a food processor and process, until the mixture resembles fine crumbs. Mix together with 1–2 tablespoons cold water to make a soft but not sticky dough. Knead lightly until smooth, then wrap in clingfilm and chill for 30 minutes.

Grease a 12-hole muffin tray. Roll out the pastry thinly on a floured surface and, using a 7.5 cm/3 inch round cutter, cut out 12 rounds. Use these to line the holes of the muffin tray, pressing the dough into the holes. Place the tray in the freezer for 5 minutes, or chill for 30 minutes.

Preheat the oven to 190°C/375°F/Gas Mark 5. Make the filling by mixing the cheeses, onions, tomatoes and basil in a bowl, then spoon the mixture into the pastry cases. In a jug, beat the eggs and milk together and season with salt and pepper.

Carefully spoon 2 tablespoons of the egg mixture into each pastry case on top of the cheese filling. Bake the tartlets for 20 minutes, or until the filling has set. Leave to cool in the tin for 5 minutes, then turn out to cool or serve warm with a fresh green salad.

OLIVE & FETA PARCELS

❁

Makes 6

1 small red pepper
1 small yellow pepper
125 g/4 oz assorted marinated
green and black olives
125 g/4 oz feta cheese
2 tbsp pine nuts, lightly toasted
6 sheets filo pastry
3 tbsp olive oil
sour cream and chive dip,
to serve

Preheat the oven to 180°C/350°F/Gas Mark 4. Preheat the grill, then line the grill rack with foil.

Cut the peppers into quarters and remove the seeds. Place skin-side up on the foil-lined grill rack and cook under the preheated grill for 10 minutes, turning occasionally, until the skins begin to blacken. Place the peppers in a polythene bag and leave until cool enough to handle, then skin and thinly slice.

Chop the olives and cut the feta cheese into small cubes. Mix together the olives, feta, sliced peppers and pine nuts.

Cut 1 sheet of filo pastry in half, then brush with a little of the oil. Place a spoonful of the olive and feta mixture about one third of the way up the pastry. Fold over the pastry and wrap to form a square parcel, encasing the filling completely.

Place this parcel in the centre of the second half of the pastry sheet. Brush the edges lightly with a little oil, bring up the corners to meet in the centre and twist them loosely to form a purse. Brush with a little more oil and repeat with the remaining filo pastry and filling.

Place the parcels on a lightly oiled baking sheet and bake in the preheated oven for 10–15 minutes until crisp and golden brown. Serve with the dip.

SPINACH, PINE NUT & MASCARPONE PIZZA

❧

Serves 2–4

For the basic pizza dough:

225 g/8 oz strong plain flour
1/2 tsp salt
1/4 tsp quick-acting dried yeast
150 ml/1/4 pint warm water
1 tbsp extra virgin olive oil

For the topping:

3 tbsp olive oil
1 large red onion, peeled
and chopped
2 garlic cloves, peeled
and finely sliced
450 g/1 lb frozen spinach, thawed
and drained
salt and freshly ground
black pepper
3 tbsp passata
125 g/4 oz mascarpone cheese
1 tbsp toasted pine nuts

Preheat the oven to 220°C/425°F/Gas Mark 7. Sift the flour and salt into a bowl and stir in the yeast. Make a well in the centre and gradually add the water and oil to form a soft dough. Knead the dough on a floured surface for about 5 minutes until smooth and elastic. Place in a lightly oiled bowl and cover with clingfilm. Leave to rise in a warm place for 1 hour.

Knock the pizza dough with your fist a few times, shape and roll out thinly on a lightly floured board. Place on a lightly floured baking sheet and lift the edge to make a little rim. Place another baking sheet into the preheated oven to heat up.

Heat half the oil in a frying pan and gently fry the onion and garlic until soft and starting to change colour.

Squeeze out any excess water from the spinach and chop finely. Add to the onion and garlic with the remaining olive oil. Season to taste with salt and pepper.

Spread the passata on the pizza dough and top with the spinach mixture. Mix the mascarpone with the pine nuts and dot over the pizza. Slide the pizza onto the hot baking sheet and bake for 15–20 minutes. Transfer to a large plate and serve immediately.

SPICY VEGETABLE SLICE

Serves 4

50 g/2 oz butter, melted
6 large or 12 small sheets filo pastry

For the filling:

2 tbsp olive oil
1 garlic clove, crushed
1 red pepper, deseeded and sliced
1 onion, chopped
50 g/2 oz button mushrooms,
wiped and quartered
1 tsp ground coriander
1 tsp paprika
175 g/6 oz cauliflower florets
75 g/3 oz French beans, trimmed
and chopped
125 g/4 oz canned chickpeas,
drained
125 g/4 oz feta cheese, crumbled
1 tbsp fresh coriander, chopped
50 g/2 oz flaked almonds
salt and freshly ground
black pepper

First, make the filling by heating the oil in a large saucepan over a medium heat. Add the garlic, red pepper and onion and fry for 3 minutes to soften. Add the mushrooms, coriander and paprika and cook for 1 minute, stirring constantly, then turn the mixture into a bowl to cool. Place the cauliflower in a large pan of boiling salted water and cook for 5 minutes. Add the beans and cook for a further 2 minutes until the vegetables are just softened, then drain well and add to the bowl with the other vegetables and add the chickpeas. Cool completely, then add the cheese and half the almonds. Season to taste with salt and pepper.

Preheat the oven to 200°C/400°F/Gas Mark 6. Brush a large baking sheet with melted butter. Unfold the filo pastry. Lay out 1 large or 2 small sheets (keeping the remaining sheets covered with a damp tea towel until you need them), overlapping on the baking sheet with the sides extending onto the work surface. Brush the pastry with melted butter. Place another layer of filo on top and repeat buttering and layering with the remaining sheets. Spoon the filling down the centre of the pastry to 3 cm/1¼ inches of the short edge. Fold the short sides over the filling and then roll up the sides to enclose the filling and make a roll. Turn the roll over and place seam-side down on the baking sheet. Brush with melted butter and sprinkle over the remaining almonds. Decorate with scraps of buttered filo pastry. Bake for about 30 minutes until golden. Serve immediately, sliced, with a fresh green salad and tomatoes.

SMOKED HADDOCK TART

Serves 6

For the shortcrust pastry:
150 g/5 oz plain flour
pinch salt
25 g/1 oz lard or white vegetable fat,
cut into small cubes
40 g/1½ oz butter or hard margarine,
cut into small cubes

For the filling:
225 g/8 oz smoked haddock,
skinned and cubed
2 large eggs, beaten
300 ml/½ pint double cream
1 tsp Dijon mustard
freshly ground black pepper
125 g/4 oz Gruyère cheese, grated
1 tbsp freshly snipped chives

To serve:
lemon wedges
tomato wedges
fresh green salad leaves

Preheat the oven to 190°C/375°F/Gas Mark 5. Sift the flour and salt into a large bowl. Add the fats and mix lightly. Using the fingertips, rub into the flour until the mixture resembles breadcrumbs. Sprinkle 1 tablespoon of cold water into the mixture and, with a knife, start bringing the dough together. (It may be necessary to use the hands for the final stage.) If the dough does not form a ball instantly, add a little more water. Put the pastry in a polythene bag and chill for at least 30 minutes.

On a lightly floured surface, roll out the pastry and use to line an 18 cm/7 inch lightly oiled quiche or flan tin. Prick the base all over with a fork and bake blind in the preheated oven for 15 minutes.

Carefully remove the pastry from the oven and brush with a little of the beaten egg. Return to the oven for a further 5 minutes.

For the filling, place the fish in the pastry case, then beat together the eggs and cream. Add the mustard, black pepper and cheese and pour over the fish. Sprinkle with the chives and bake for 35–40 minutes until the filling is golden brown and set in the centre. Serve hot or cold with the lemon and tomato wedges and salad leaves.

SMOKED MACKEREL VOL-AU-VENTS

❀

Serves 1–2

350 g/12 oz prepared puff pastry
1 small egg, beaten
2 tsp sesame seeds
225 g/8 oz peppered smoked mackerel, skinned and chopped
5 cm/2 inch piece cucumber
4 tbsp soft cream cheese
2 tbsp cranberry sauce
1 tbsp freshly chopped dill
1 tbsp finely grated lemon zest
dill sprigs, to garnish
mixed salad leaves, to serve

Preheat the oven to 230°C/450°F/Gas Mark 8. Roll the pastry out on a lightly floured surface and, using a 9 cm/3^1/$_2$ inch fluted cutter, cut out 12 rounds. Using a 1 cm/^{1}/$_2$ inch cutter, mark a lid in the centre of each round. Place on a damp baking sheet and brush the rounds with a little beaten egg.

Sprinkle the pastry with the sesame seeds and bake in the preheated oven for 10–12 minutes until golden brown and well risen.

Transfer the vol-au-vents to a chopping board and, when cool enough to touch, carefully remove the lids with a small sharp knife. Scoop out any uncooked pastry from the inside of each vol-au-vent, then return to the oven for 5–8 minutes to dry out. Remove and allow to cool.

Flake the mackerel into small pieces and reserve. Peel the cucumber if desired, cut into very small dice and add to the mackerel.

Beat the soft cream cheese with the cranberry sauce, dill and lemon zest. Stir in the mackerel and cucumber and use to fill the vol-au-vents. Place the lids on top and garnish with dill sprigs.

SAUVIGNON CHICKEN & MUSHROOM FILO PIE

❧

Serves 4

1 onion, peeled and chopped
1 leek, trimmed and chopped
225 ml/8 fl oz chicken stock
3 x 175 g/6 oz chicken breasts
150 ml/¼ pint dry white wine
1 bay leaf
175 g/6 oz baby button mushrooms
2 tbsp plain flour
1 tbsp freshly chopped tarragon
salt and freshly ground
black pepper
fresh parsley sprig, to garnish
seasonal vegetables, to serve

For the topping:

75 g/3 oz (about 5 sheets) filo pastry
1 tbsp sunflower oil
1 tsp sesame seeds

Preheat the oven to 190°C/375°F/Gas Mark 5. Put the onion and leek in a heavy-based saucepan with 125 ml/4 fl oz of the stock. Bring to the boil, cover and simmer for 5 minutes, then uncover and cook until all the stock has evaporated and the vegetables are tender.

Cut the chicken into bite-size cubes. Add to the pan with the remaining stock, the wine and the bay leaf. Cover and gently simmer for 5 minutes. Add the mushrooms and simmer for a further 5 minutes.

Blend the flour with 3 tablespoons of cold water. Stir into the pan and cook, stirring all the time, until the sauce has thickened. Stir the tarragon into the sauce and season with salt and pepper. Spoon the mixture into a 1.2 litre/2 pint pie dish, discarding the bay leaf.

Lightly brush a sheet of filo pastry with a little of the oil. Crumple the pastry slightly. Arrange on top of the filling. Repeat with the remaining filo sheets and oil, then sprinkle the top of the pie with the sesame seeds. Bake the pie on the middle shelf of the preheated oven for 20 minutes until the filo pastry topping is golden and crisp. Garnish with a sprig of parsley. Serve the pie immediately with the seasonal vegetables.

CORNISH PASTIES

꧁꧂

Makes 8

For the pastry:

350 g/12 oz self-raising flour
75 g/3 oz butter or margarine
75 g/3 oz lard or white vegetable fat
salt and freshly ground
black pepper

For the filling:

550 g/1 lb 3 oz braising steak,
very finely chopped
1 large onion, peeled and
finely chopped
1 large potato, peeled and diced
200 g/7 oz swede, peeled and diced
3 tbsp Worcestershire sauce
1 small egg, beaten, to glaze

To garnish:

tomato slices or wedges
fresh parsley sprigs

Preheat the oven to 180°C/350°F/Gas Mark 4, about 15 minutes before required. To make the pastry, sift the flour into a large bowl and add the fats, chopped into small pieces. Rub the fats and flour together until the mixture resembles coarse breadcrumbs. Season to taste with salt and pepper and mix again. Add about 2 tablespoons of cold water, a little at a time, and mix until the mixture comes together to form a firm but pliable dough. Turn onto a lightly floured surface, knead until smooth, then wrap and chill in the refrigerator for 30 minutes.

To make the filling, put the braising steak in a large bowl with the onion. Add the potato and swede to the bowl, together with the Worcestershire sauce and salt and pepper. Mix well.

Divide the dough into 8 balls and roll each ball into a round about 25.5 cm/10 inches across. Divide the filling between the rounds of pastry. Wet the edges of the pastry, then fold over the filling. Pinch the edges to seal.

Transfer the pasties to a lightly oiled baking sheet. Make a couple of small holes in each pasty and brush with beaten egg. Cook in the preheated oven for 15 minutes, remove and brush again with the egg. Return to the oven for a further 15–20 minutes until golden. Cool slightly, garnish with tomato and parsley and serve.

CARIBBEAN EMPANADAS

Serves 4–6

175 g/6 oz lean fresh beef mince
175 g/6 oz lean fresh pork mince
1 onion, peeled and finely chopped
1 Scotch bonnet chilli, deseeded
and finely chopped
1 small red pepper,
deseeded and finely chopped
1/2 tsp ground cloves
1 tsp ground cinnamon
1/2 tsp ground allspice
1 tsp sugar
1 tbsp tomato purée
6 tbsp water
700 g/1 1/2 lb prepared shortcrust
pastry (*see* page 24)
melted butter, for brushing
lime wedges, to garnish
mango relish, to serve

Preheat the oven to 200°C/400°F/Gas Mark 6, 15 minutes before baking.

Place the mince in a nonstick frying pan and cook, stirring, for 5–8 minutes, or until sealed. Break up any lumps with a wooden spoon. Add the onion, chilli and red pepper together with the spices and cook, stirring, for 10 minutes, or until the onion has softened. Sprinkle in the sugar.

Blend the tomato purée with the water and stir into the meat. Bring to the boil, then reduce the heat and simmer for 10 minutes. Allow to cool.

Roll the pastry out on a lightly floured surface and cut into 10 cm/ 4 inch rounds. Place a spoonful of the meat mixture onto the centre of each pastry round and brush the edges with water. Fold over, encasing the filling to form small pasties.

Brush with melted butter and bake in the preheated oven for 20 minutes until golden. Garnish and serve with the mango relish.

BEEF & RED WINE PIE

❧

Serves 4

700 g/1½ lb stewing beef, cubed
4 tbsp seasoned plain flour
2 tbsp sunflower oil
2 onions, peeled and chopped
2 garlic cloves, peeled and crushed
1 tbsp freshly chopped thyme
300 ml/½ pint red wine
150 ml/¼ pint beef stock
1–2 tsp Worcestershire sauce
2 tbsp tomato ketchup
2 bay leaves
knob butter
225 g/8 oz button mushrooms
1 quantity quick flaky pastry
(see page 26), chilled
beaten egg or milk, to glaze
parsley sprig, to garnish

Preheat the oven to 200°C/400°F/Gas Mark 6. Toss the beef cubes in the seasoned flour.

Heat the oil in a large heavy-based frying pan. Fry the beef in batches for about 5 minutes until golden brown. Return all of the beef to the pan and add the onions, garlic and thyme. Fry for about 10 minutes, stirring occasionally. If the beef begins to stick, add a little water. Add the red wine and stock and bring to the boil. Stir in the Worcestershire sauce, tomato ketchup and bay leaves.

Cover and simmer on a very low heat for about 1 hour until the beef is tender. Heat the butter and gently sauté the mushrooms until golden brown. Add to the stew. Simmer uncovered for a further 15 minutes. Remove the bay leaves. Spoon the beef into a 1.1 litre/2 pint pie dish and reserve.

Roll out the pastry on a lightly floured surface. Cut out the lid to be 5 mm/¼ inch wider than the dish. Brush the rim with beaten egg and lay the lid on top. Press to seal, then knock the edges with the back of a knife.

Cut a slit in the lid and brush with the beaten egg or milk to glaze. Bake in the preheated oven for 30 minutes, or until golden brown. Garnish with the sprig of parsley and serve immediately.

INDEX

Index